FOUR POINT

Listening and Speaking

INTRO

ENGLISH FOR ACADEMIC PURPOSES

KEITH S. FOLSE
University of Central Florida

ROBYN BRINKS LOCKWOOD
Stanford University

Series Editor: KEITH S. FOLSE

Ann Arbor
University of Michigan Press

∞ Printed on acid-free paper

ISBN-13: 978-0-472-03472-7

2014   2013   2012   2011   4   3   2   1

Contents

Acknowledgments

Robyn would like to thank Keith Folse, her co-author and series editor, for his valuable feedback and input, and Kelly Sippell, for her constant support and dedication to producing strong English language materials. Personal thanks to the original Brinks clan, Virgil, June, and Tim, the next generation, Darrin and Nathan, and the newest members, Sara and Andrew, for being as proud of me as I am of all of them. And, to my husband, John, for continually giving me all open desk, table, and floor space for my page proofs.

The publisher, series editor, and authors would like to thank the educational professionals whose reviews helped shape the Four Point series, particularly those from these institutions: Auburn University, Boston University CELOP, Central Piedmont Community College, Colorado State University, Daytona Beach Community College, Duke University, Durham Technical College, Georgia State University, Harding University, Hillsborough Community College, Northern Virginia Community College–Alexandria Campus, Oregon State University, University of California–San Diego, University of Nevada at Las Vegas, University of North Carolina–Charlotte, and Valencia Community College.

Grateful acknowledgment is made to the following authors, publishers, and individuals for permission to reprint copyrighted or previously published materials.

Library of Congress for photos of John F. Kennedy and Richard M. Nixon.

Thinkstock.com for all other photos.

Every effort has been made to contact the copyright holders for permission to reprint borrowed material. We regret any oversights that may have occurred and will rectify them in future printings of this book.

The University of Michigan Press thanks: Gabriela Beres, Pat Grimes, Scott Ham, Badria Jazairi, Sheryl Leicher, Claudia Leo, Heather Newman, Morgan Peterson, and Laurel Stroud for contributing their talent to the audio.

The University of Michigan Press thanks: Anna Dean, Kelsey Dean, Angie Feak, Scott Ham, Adam Jazairi, Sheryl Leicher, and Serena Wu for contributing their talent to the videos.

Series Overview

Four Point is a six-volume series designed for English language learners whose primary goal is to succeed in an academic setting. While grammar points and learning strategies are certainly important, academic English language learners (ELLs) need skills-based books that focus on the four primary skills of reading, writing, listening, and speaking in a realistic, integrated format, as well as the two primary language bases of vocabulary and grammar. To this end, the *Four Point* series offers a unique combination of instructional material and activities that truly require students to read, write, speak, and listen in a multitude of combinations.

Four Point has three English for Academic Purposes (EAP) levels. While academic listening and speaking skills are covered in one volume and academic reading and writing are covered in another, *all four skills are integrated throughout all books,* so a given task may focus on speaking and listening but have a reading and/or writing component to it as well.

Developing the Four Skills in *Four Point*

The series covers the four academic skills of reading, writing, listening, and speaking, while providing reinforcement and systematic recycling of key vocabulary issues and further exposure to grammar issues. The goal of this series is to help students improve their ability in each of these four critical skills and thereby enable the students to have sufficient English to succeed in their final academic setting, whether it be community college, college, or university.

Many ELLs report great difficulties upon entering their academic courses after they leave the safe haven of their English class with other nonnative speakers and their sympathetic and caring ESL teachers. Their academic instructors speak quickly, give long reading assignments due the next day, deliver classroom lectures and interactions at rapid, native speed, and sometimes balk at the excessive errors in their ELLs' writing. In sum, the ELL who has gone through a sheltered classroom setting is in for a rather rude awakening in a new learning situation where English is taken for granted and no one seems to understand or care much about the new reality of the dilemmas facing ELLs. Through these materials, we hope to lessen the shock of such an awakening.

The activities in *Four Point* achieve the goal of helping ELLs experience what life beyond the ESL classroom is like while they are still in a sheltered classroom. This chart explains some of the activities in *Four Point*:

Reading	Listening
Students will read longer, more difficult readings on interesting academic topics that represent the array of interests in a classroom. Extensive pleasure reading is good, but ELLs need practice for the type of reading they will find in their academic course books as well. Strategies introduced in the books will help develop the skills necessary to read challenging academic material.	Students will have to listen to informational conversations, group discussions, and lectures to not only pick out details and facts but also practice picking up on speaker opinions and organizational patterns. Students will also gain experience listening to multiple native speakers at the same time.
Writing	Speaking
Students will write both short and long assignments. Special emphasis is given to the academic writing skills of paraphrasing, summarizing, and synthesizing.	Students will practice both short and long speaking activities and thereby develop their speaking fluency, an area often overlooked in many ESL books. Students will also practice encouraging communication, politely interrupting, and adding speech to another speaker's ideas on the spot.

Maximizing Coverage of the Two Primary Language Bases

ESL materials have come a long way from the old days of equating repetitive grammar drills for speaking practice or copying sentences for writing practice. However, in the ensuing shift from focus on language to focus on communication, very little was developed to address the needs of academic ELLs who need to do much more in English than engage in conversations about daily events, fill out job applications, or read short pieces of text for pleasure. It was the proverbial "baby being thrown out with the bath water" as emphasis on grammar and vocabulary was downplayed. However, in order to participate in academic settings, our ELLs certainly need focused activities to develop and then maintain their use of vocabulary and grammar. Toward this end, the *Four*

Point series provides further exposure of key grammar issues without overt practice activities.

More important, these books focus very heavily on vocabulary because ELLs realize that they are way behind their native-speaker counterparts when it comes to vocabulary. Each book highlights between 125–150 key vocabulary items, including individual words, compound words, phrasal verbs, short phrases, idioms, metaphors, collocations, and longer set lexical phrases. In learning vocabulary, the two most important features are frequency of retrievals (i.e., in exercises) and the spacing between these retrievals. Spaced rehearsal is accomplished in two ways. First, after words appear in a textbook, they will reappear multiple times afterward. Second, interactive web-based exercises provide more than ample opportunities for ELLs to practice their vocabulary learning through spaced rehearsals at the student's convenience (www.press.umich.edu/esl/compsite/4Point/).

General Overview of Units

Each of the books is divided into six units with numerous activities within each unit. The material in each of the volumes could be covered in ten to twelve weeks, but this number is flexible depending on the students and the teacher, and the depth to which the material is practiced.

Using the Exercises in This Book

Each unit includes three listening passages within a field of academic study (i.e., one informational conversation or discussion, one group discussion, and one lecture). The exercises accompanying the passages are meant to strengthen a range of listening and speaking skills, notably:

- understanding main ideas
- comprehending details
- understanding classroom discourse
- using academic language functions
- recognizing signal words and phrases
- developing vocabulary
- synthesizing information

In addition to more general listening comprehension tasks, most units include a specific listening focus, such as listening for facts, listening for cues, or listening for advice. The lectures range in length from approximately three to five minutes. In addition, most of the other tasks are between two and four minutes, offering practice with longer, connected discourse that students need to build listening comprehension skills. Lectures and other material are provided on the audio CD packaged with the book. Six video clips can be found online at www.press.umich.edu/esl/compsite/4Point/.

Pre-Listening Activities

A range of pre-listening discussion questions is included; each has the purpose of activating prior knowledge about and generating interest in the topics in the unit. Often these questions provide opportunities for students to anticipate content and, therefore, may be revisited throughout the unit. All of the pre-listening tasks lead to pair or small group discussions.

Note-Taking Strategies

Each unit introduces a note-taking strategy, allowing students to develop a repertoire of techniques to choose from as they take notes or organize the notes later. As students preferences vary, it is important to supply them with options. It is certainly possible that students can draw on formats that work particularly well for them in one unit as they practice and develop their note-taking skills in another.

Other types of strategies and skills—those related to listening, speaking, and vocabulary—are highlighted at various points throughout the units. Each appears in a display box with a short explanation.

Listening Activities

Each note-taking activity in a unit is followed by main idea and detailed comprehension questions. The main idea questions serve to help students summarize ideas from their notes. Students can listen to the lecture again as they complete the multiple choice questions for Check Your Understanding: Details. The listening passage allows students to practice the strategy and/or hear the signal words or phrases in use.

Vocabulary Activities

Vocabulary Power activities appear once in each unit. The words chosen for these tasks are ones that may appear in a variety of academic settings. These activities serve to further check students' comprehension of the lecture. These words are likely to be useful to the students as they move on to the extensive speaking activities at the end of each unit: the Rapid Vocabulary Review, which focuses on synonyms and combinations and associations, and the Vocabulary Log. Students could also be asked to listen to portions of the lecture again to discover if they recognize the words used in context.

In-Class and Out-of-Class Interactions/Classroom Discourse

In addition to the lectures, each unit includes activities based on the in-class interactions students are likely to encounter in post-secondary classrooms. Throughout the units, students participate in group activities that allow them to use the speaking phrases taught in the unit. Other activities include information gaps, rankings, and in-depth discussions. Each unit contains a Making Contact activity designed to put students into interactive situations with native speakers and to research phrases used in their discipline.

In addition, the audio includes several features of everyday language that are designed to help make the audio and video more realistic for students. For example, the interactions and lectures include some false starts, error corrections, and reductions. Also, in the attempt to help students understand more than professional native speakers, the audio CD features fluent non-native speakers in the role of a TA (teaching assistant) to replicate university settings, as a participant in a lecture, and as the museum tour guide.

Six video clips are provided on the companion website (**www.press.umich. edu/esl/compsite/4Point/**) to analyze for language, tone, and nonverbal cues as well as to generate discussion on academic listening and speaking tasks. Throughout the interaction, the students use many of the phrases and employ the strategies taught in the unit—and, in some cases, not using the best communication strategies. ELLs will have the opportunity to hear the phrases used in a natural conversation, practice their listening skills, analyze verbal and nonverbal communication skills of the students, and think critically about and discuss the interaction with their classmates. Questions in the book require students to listen for certain phrases and identify what they mean; to notice the tone of voice and think about how it changes the dynamics of a discussion; to recognize the influence of nonverbal communication by increasing their awareness of facial expressions, gestures, and other cues; and compile all of these ideas into an analytical discussion about the interaction in the video.

Reading Tasks

Each unit includes a reading generally used as the impetus for more extensive speaking activities and as a way to practice the strategies. As such, they do not include detailed comprehension questions. As the topics in the units are recent, the instructor could easily supplement a unit with current online readings.

Synthesizing: Projects and Presentations

The summative task for each unit includes four projects that relate to the topic and encourage practice of the listening and speaking concepts. Students prepare projects and presentations based on what they have learned via the lectures, readings, discussions, or online or library research. For group projects, students should be given adequate time to clarify group roles and to work on their projects.

Rapid Vocabulary Review and Vocabulary Log

A vocabulary review task appears at the end of each unit and gives students another opportunity to check their understanding of key words. The correct answer is a synonym or brief definition. Crucial to the vocabulary acquisition process is the initial noticing of unknown vocabulary. ELLs must notice the vocabulary in some way, and this noticing then triggers awareness of the item and draws the learner's attention to the word in all subsequent encounters, whether the word is read in a passage or heard in a conversation or lecture. To facilitate noticing and then multiple retrievals of new vocabulary, we have included a chart listing 25 key vocabulary items at the end of each unit. This Vocabulary Log has three columns and requires students to provide a definition or translation in the second column and then an original example or note about usage in the third column. As demonstrated in *Vocabulary Myths* (Folse 2004, University of Michigan Press), there is no research showing that a definition is better than a translation or vice-versa, so we suggest that you let ELLs decide which one they prefer. After all, this log is each student's individual vocabulary notebook, so students should use whatever information is helpful to them and that will help them remember and use the vocabulary item. If the log information is not deemed useful, the learner will not review this material—which defeats the whole purpose of keeping the notebook. In the third column, students can use the word in a phrase or sentence, or they can also add usage information about the word such as *usually negative, very formal sounding,* or *used only with the word* launch.

1 Architecture: Applied Science

An applied science is one in which people use science to do something practical. Architecture is often considered an applied science because it involves using science to construct something that people use, such as buildings. Architects must think about design so the building looks nice, while also considering technical aspects to make the building safe and functional. This unit explores architecture as an art and as a science.

Part 1: Architecture as an Art and a Science

Pre-Listening Activities

Writing a definition for the word *architecture* can be difficult because it involves both art (or design) and science (or engineering). Some architects like the blend because they have a chance to be both creative and practical. Even for the earliest works of architecture, the blend of art and science was a part of the field. Answer these questions with a partner.

1. Which part of architecture do you think you would like better—art or science? Why?

   _____

   _____

   _____

2. What types of buildings would you want to develop?

   _____

   _____

   _____

3. What kinds of things do you think an architect needs to think about for the design? For the science?

   _____

   _____

   _____

Strategy: Listening for and Giving Encouragement in Discussion

In English, it is important to notice when a speaker is encouraging you to participate. There are several strategies a speaker may use to ask you to participate. These strategies are good to use when you are the speaker too.

Ask Questions

- when you can't hear the speaker

  Excuse me. I could not hear what you said about that building. Will you say it again?

- when you can't understand the speaker

  Excuse me. I don't know what kind of architecture that is. Can you explain it?

- when you want to make sure you understood (especially with names and numbers)

  When did you say that happened? 1988?

- when you need more information

  I have not heard of that architect. How do you spell that name?

- when you want more information

  Where is that building?

Make Requests

- for more information

  That type of architecture is new for me. It's interesting. I'd like to learn more.

  Can you spell that?

- for something to be repeated

  Would you repeat the question, please?

  Will you say that again?

- for an example

  What is an example?

Paraphrase

- when you want to make sure you understand

  So he's excluding bridges as a work of art, right?

  Did you say _____?

Use Voice Fillers

Hmmm.	Go on.	Really?
Oh.	Yes. Yeah.	Tell me more?
Wow.	Unh uh.	Cool/That's cool.
That's interesting.	Right.	

Pronunciation Note: **Intonation** is the pitch—or the rising and falling of the voice when someone is speaking. In English, sometimes a person's pitch goes up. Other times, a person's pitch falls. When asking questions that that have a yes or no answer, use **rising** intonation. When asking *wh-* questions, use **falling** intonation. If you use the opposite intonation, the speaker might think you are being rude, misunderstanding the information, or expressing a different emotion.

Yes-No Questions	Wh- Questions
Do you live near here?	Where do you live?
Is tomorrow's test on both chapters?	What is tomorrow's test on?
Have you visited the Eiffel Tower?	Which famous sites have you visited?

Pronunciation Note: Some voice fillers can use rising intonation as well, making them sound like a question and encouraging the speaker to repeat or give more information. Review the list of fillers given.

Listening for and Giving Encouragement in Discussion

Work with a small group. Divide the reading on pages 5–6 into equal parts. Imagine you are the instructor discussing your research with students. Read your part of the reading to the other members of your group, and be prepared for them to be encouraging in the discussion by using the strategies in the box on pages 3–4. Take turns being the instructor and the student. Use this space to take notes while your classmates are the instructors.

_____

_____

_____

Reading

Reading about Architectural Achievements

Read about the Historic American Building Survey (HABS), the Historic American Engineering Record (HAER), and some architectural achievements. Then look for photos of each online.

Overview

(1) The Historic American Buildings Survey (HABS) and the Historic American Engineering Record (HAER) collections are among the largest and most heavily used in the Prints and Photographs Division of the Library of Congress. Since 2000, documentation from the Historic American Landscapes Survey (HALS) has been added to the holdings. The collections document achievements in architecture, engineering, and design in the United States and its territories through a comprehensive range of building types and engineering technologies, including examples as diverse as the Pueblo of Acoma, houses, windmills, one-room schools, the Golden Gate Bridge, and buildings designed by Frank Lloyd Wright. Administered since 1933 through cooperative agreements with the National Park Service, the Library of Congress, and the private sector, ongoing programs of the National Park Service have recorded America's man-made environment in multiformat surveys comprising more than 556,900 measured drawings, large-format photographs, and written histories for more than 38,600 historic structures and sites dating from Pre-Columbian times to the twentieth century.

Golden Gate Bridge, San Francisco, California

(2) An international icon of American engineering genius, the Golden Gate Bridge opened in 1937 and remains one of the longest suspension bridges in the world. The main span of 4,200 feet crosses the turbulent waters at the entrance to San Francisco Bay. Chief engineer Joseph B. Strauss started the construction project in 1933.

Ritter Ranch barn, Dolores vicinity, Colorado

(3) This wooden dairy barn, built in 1918, is the largest outbuilding on the Ritter Ranch, once the most technologically advanced ranch in the Lower Dolores Valley of Colorado. Divided crosswise by a central breezeway on the first floor and lengthwise by two rows of wooden poles supporting the roof, the barn has an airy and peaceful hayloft that contrasts sharply with the complicated machinery of the work area below.

First Church of Christ, Congregational (Meetinghouse), Farmington, Connecticut

(4) The First Church of Christ is Connecticut's best surviving example of a colonial-era meeting house. Built in 1771 by Captain Judah Woodruff, who also built many of the houses in Farmington, the church has undergone only minor alterations and still retains its side entrance; graceful, tall steeple; and plain, boxy styling. The church has played an important role in the town since it was built. In 1841, for instance, the African captives from the Spanish slave ship *Amistad* lived in Farmington and attended the First Church of Christ for several months while awaiting passage back to Africa.

The Arsenal, New Castle, Delaware

(5) The U.S. government built this arsenal in 1809 under threat of war with Britain. Originally a one-story building with a wagon entrance at each end to help with the storage and distribution of arms, the Old Arsenal played an important role in both the War of 1812 and the Mexican War of 1846–48. It also housed the garrison from nearby Fort Delaware when that fort burned in 1831. The second story and cupola date from the 1850s, when the building was converted into a public school.

Adapted from Library of Congress, *American Memory,* "Built in America."

Listening 1: Getting the Information You Need

Listening for Information

The listening passage is a conversation between a student and a teaching assistant. They are discussing the definition of architecture. The student needs more information about the content and uses several strategies to learn the information. As you listen to the conversation, write answers to the questions.

Listening for Information

1. What questions does the student ask the TA to encourage discussion?

   _____

   _____

   _____

2. What is the purpose of each of his questions? In other words, what is he trying to accomplish with each question?

   _____

   _____

   _____

3. What requests does he make?

   _____

   _____

   _____

4. List any voice fillers you hear.

   _____

   _____

   _____

Speaking

Greetings

Before starting a conversation or discussion, most people begin with a greeting. This sometimes breaks the ice and helps the interaction seem friendly and open. There are many greetings in English, and some are more formal than others.

GREETINGS

Formal	Informal
Hello.	Hi.
Good morning/afternoon/evening.	Hey.
How are you?	How you doing?
It's nice to see you.	What's up?
It's been a long time.	Long time, no see.
How have you been?	How's it going?
How are things going?	What's new?

Using Greetings

Think about greetings, and answer these questions with a partner. Then share your ideas with the class.

1. Would you greet each of these people formally or informally?

   a. your English teacher _____

   b. an instructor in your department _____

   c. the department chairperson _____

   d. your roommate _____

   e. a relative _____

   f. a cashier at the bookstore _____

   g. a new classmate who sits next to you in class _____

2. What greetings do you frequently use every day? Add other greetings to the list on page 8.

_____

_____

3. What things affect the greeting and/or the response? Does the place or time of the interaction matter? Does the formality of the greeting affect the response?

_____

_____

 Making Contact

Choose three greetings from the list on page 8, and greet three different English speakers. Take notes on the greeting you used, the response you received, and the details of the interaction (person's status, age, and gender, the time of day, and the location). Follow the example. Be prepared to discuss your data with the class.

Your Greeting	The Person's Response	Details of the Interaction
Hi.	Hi.	classmates, same age, male, morning, hallway

Part 2: Architecture as an Art

Pre-Listening Activities

What do you know about architecture? Although schools and universities offer classes about architecture, most people do not know much about it. They do not realize the science and engineering that goes into making a building. However, many buildings are recognizable and remembered for their unique appearance. The design is the creative side of architecture. Answer these questions with a partner.

1. Do you recognize these buildings? What are they? What city or country are they in?

_____

_____

_____

2. What do you like and dislike about each building?

_____

_____

_____

3. What is one of your favorite buildings—either one you have seen or one you have visited? Why do you like it?

_____

_____

_____

Strategy: Listening for and Determining the Speaker's Feelings

In English, speakers use different ways to express their feelings.

Language

Sometimes you can tell how someone feels by the words they choose to use or by extra words they add before a descriptive word.

> I'm **so happy** we got to see the Sydney Opera House.
>
> The Guggenheim Museum is **incredibly beautiful.**
>
> The airport was **huge!**

Tone

You can also tell how a person feels by the particular tone of voice he or she uses. A person can sound happy, confused, or upset, or convey any other emotion.

Nonverbal Communication

Sometimes speakers convey feelings without saying anything at all.

- **Facial expressions** (smiling, frowning, open or closed eyes, open or closed mouth, raised eyebrows)
- **Eye contact** (direct or indirect)
- **Posture** (leaning forward, sliding down in the chair, standing or sitting straight)
- **Head movement** (nodding, shaking, tipping)
- **Gestures** (hand movements, symbols)

Notice how many speakers combine language, tone, and nonverbal communication to make their communication more powerful. Recognizing these things will help you understand others and help you better convey how you feel.

Pronunciation Note: **Tone** can also be conveyed through emphasis on certain words or saying vowel sounds longer than other sounds in the word.

> I **just** **lo-ooove** the design of the Beijing National Stadium.
>
> I **simply** **can-not** understand what that architect was thinking when he designed that museum!
>
> The airport was **so-ooo** big that it was **very** overwhelming.

Listening for and Expressing Feelings

Write three sentences about buildings you can think of or are familiar with. Say them to a partner, expressing yourself clearly in English. Use a strategy or combination of strategies from the box on page 11. Can your partner tell how you feel about the buildings?

Your Sentences

_____

_____

_____

Speaking

I'm Sorry and *Excuse Me*

Two common phrases in English are *I'm sorry* and *Excuse me*. They are used often but for different reasons. Recognizing the differences will help you understand what other people mean and will make your own purpose clear when you are the speaker.

USE *I'M SORRY* TO . . .

apologize for forgetting or not knowing a person's name
apologize for hurting a person's feelings
apologize for interrupting
ask for repetition
correct something said incorrectly
express sadness for hurting a person physically
express sympathy for someone's situation
regret being late, saying the wrong thing, losing something
show you are sincere and accept responsibility for your actions
turn down an invitation

USE *EXCUSE ME* TO . . .

ask someone for a favor
be formal in academic or professional places
be polite after coughing, clearing your throat, sneezing, etc.
be polite with people you do not know well
get someone's attention
interrupt a speaker nicely
leave a room, conversation, group, etc.

Analyzing the Situation

Work with a partner. Read each situation, and decide what you would say or do in each situation. Include *I'm sorry* or *Excuse me*. Choose two situations, and write a dialogue for each on a separate sheet of paper.

1. You're at the library, and you need to know what time it is so you won't miss your architecture class. You want to ask the student sitting at the next table. _____

2. The teacher is collecting the design homework assignment, but you are not finished with it. You want to explain to the teacher. _____

3. Your pen ran out of ink during an office hour with your English teacher. You need to borrow a pen to finish taking notes about the advice for your building design. _____

4. You're at a party talking with a friend when you see a classmate from your architecture class come into the room. You want to go say hello. _____

5. You are unable to attend a party for your friend who won the school's design contest. You need to tell your friend you will not be there. _____

6. You dropped water on your roommate's model building. You want to tell your roommate what happened. _____

Listening 2: Managing Group Dynamics

Listening in Groups (Video)

Listen to the students work together to decide on the type of building to report on for their architecture class. Discuss the questions in a small group.

Focus on Language

1. What greetings do the students use? Refer to those given on page 8.

   _____

   _____

2. What can you guess about their relationships based on their greetings?

   _____

   _____

3. Make a list of when you hear the phrases *I'm sorry* and *Excuse me*. What does each one mean? Do you think there are other times students could use the phrases?

   _____

   _____

   _____

4. Write any phrases or idioms that you are not familiar with. Discuss what they mean and in what type of interactions they are appropriate.

   _____

   _____

Focus on Tone

1. Describe the tone and emotion used by each member of the group.

   _____

   _____

2. How can you tell how each person is feeling?

   _____

   _____

3. Is each person's tone appropriate for the situation? Why or why not?

_____

_____

Focus on Nonverbal Communication

1. What nonverbal cues are used to show how each member of the group feels about ideas from other group members?

_____

_____

2. Were any of these inappropriate? Why or why not?

_____

_____

3. Which student do you think is the best at nonverbal communication? Is this good or bad for the interaction?

_____

_____

_____

Summary

1. What strategies do the students use to encourage communication?

_____

_____

_____

2. Which student uses the best combination of words, tone, and nonverbal communication? Support your answer.

_____

_____

_____

_____

3. Who would you most want to work with? Why? Who would you rather not work with? Why?

_____

_____

_____

_____

Information Gap

One interesting feature of architectural design is its height—how many floors and how many feet high. Because designs vary, it is not always the buildings with the most stories that are the highest in feet.

Work with a partner to complete the chart. Person A has Chart 1 on page 17, and Person B has Chart 2 on page 18. Work back to back to complete the information. Ask for information and for clarification if you need to.

CHART 1

Ranking	Building	Stories	Height (in feet)	Year Completed
1	Burj Khalifa (Dubai, United Arab Emirates)	162		2010
2	Taipei 101 Tower (Taiwan)	101	1,671	2004
3		101	1,614	2008
4	International Commerce Centre (Hong Kong)		1588	2010
5		88	1,483	1998
6	Nanjing Greenland Financial Center	66	1,476	
7	Willis Tower (Chicago, United States)	108	1,451	1974
8	Guangzhou West Tower (Guangzhou, China)		1,435	2010
9		88	1,380	1999
10	Two International Finance Centre (Hong Kong)	88		2003
11	Trump International Hotel (Chicago, United States)	96	1,362	
12	CITIC Plaza (Guanzhou, China)		1,283	1997
13	Shun Hing Square (Shenzhen, China)	69	1,260	1996
14	Empire State Building (New York, United States)	102	1,250	
15	Central Plaza (Hong Kong)	78		1992

Data from www.emporis.com/en/bu/sk/st/tp/wo/.

CHART 2

Ranking	Building	Stories	Height (in feet)	Year Completed
1	Khalifa (Dubai, United Arab Emirates)	162	2,717	
2	Taipei 101 Tower (Taiwan)	101	1,671	2004
3	Shanghai World Financial Center (China)		1,614	2008
4		108	1588	2010
5	Petronas Towers 1 and 2 (Kuala Lumpur, Malaysia)	88	1,483	
6		66		2010
7	Willis Tower (Chicago, United States)		1,451	1974
8	Guangzhou West Tower (Guangzhou, China)	103	1,435	2010
9	Jin Mao Building (Shanghai, China)	88	1,380	1999
10		88	1, 362	2003
11	Trump International Hotel (Chicago, United States)	96		2009
12	CITIC Plaza (Guanzhou, China)	80	1,283	1997
13	Shun Hing Square (Shenzhen, China)		1,260	1996
14	Empire State Building (New York, United States)	102		1931
15	Central Plaza (Hong Kong)	78	1,227	

Data from www.emporis.com/en/bu/sk/st/tp/wo/.

Part 3: Architecture as a Science

Pre-Listening Activities

Most people notice what a building looks like when it is built. Not everyone thinks about the technical work that goes into constructing a building. Architecture includes aspects of science that not only make the building visually appealing but also functional to the people who will later use the building. Answer these questions with a partner.

1. What kinds of technical details do you think are involved in constructing a new building?

   _____

   _____

   _____

2. What are some jobs that involve the science of building?

   _____

   _____

3. Do you think you would like working on the scientific aspects of a building? Why or why not?

   _____

   _____

   _____

4. What types of practical things might conflict with designing the most beautiful building in the world?

   _____

   _____

Strategy: Listening for and Using Time Signal Words and Phrases

Speakers often use signal words to let you know the time something happened or will happen. It is a good idea to notice these because it helps you organize the content.

Time Signal Words and Phrases

- *first, second, third, another, next*

  To major in architecture, **first,** talk to your advisor.

  The **second** thing you should do is enroll in the Introduction to Architecture course.

  Third, talk to a professional architect to learn more about the job.

  Another thing to do is look at Architecture 161.

- *before, during, after/afterward, later*

  Before changing your major, you should talk to your advisor.

  The instructor will talk about the history of architecture **during** the lecture.

  There will be an examination **after** the course.

  We'll have a review session **later.**

- *in the past, in the future, used to be, currently, now*

  In the past, architects were responsible for all aspects of a building.

  No one knows how the study of architecture will change **in the future.**

  It **used to be** that one architect managed the whole project.

  Currently, some architects specialize on one aspect.

- *meanwhile*

  One architect is working on the design. **Meanwhile,** his partner is working on the measurements.

- *yesterday, today, tomorrow*

  The material we covered **yesterday** will be covered on the test.

  There is a study session **today.**

  Be prepared for the test **tomorrow.**

What others can you think of to add to the lists?

Using Time Signal Words and Phrases in a Story

Write a story, and add a few details about one of your classes. Add time signal words so your classmates can tell when things happen. Read your story in a small group.

_____

_____

_____

_____

_____

_____

_____

_____

_____

_____

_____

_____

_____

_____

_____

_____

_____

_____

_____

Note-Taking

Strategy: Using an Abbreviation Log

Each student should have his or her own log of abbreviations. The abbreviations you choose should be used consistently for all your notes in all your classes. This will save you time. There are some common abbreviations used by native English speakers that you can use, or you can use your own. Use whatever will be easy for you to remember and use. A copy of your log should be in each of your notebooks or with you whenever you take notes. It can be handwritten or typed so you can add to it.

A sample log for the time signal words may look like this:

first = 1st	second = 2nd	third = 3rd
before = b/f	during = d-ing	after = aft afterward = a/w
past = ←	present = ↑	future = →
meanwhile = m/w		
yesterday = ydy	today = tdy	tomorrow = tom

You'll have a chance to practice abbreviations for time signal words and phrase in the lecture. Thinking about them before will help you to use them and miss less of what the instructor is saying.

Developing an Abbreviation Log

Write an abbreviation for some of these commonly used words in English, and share them with a partner.

because _____

falling _____

hour _____

large _____

medium _____

minute _____

rising _____

small _____

without _____

Make a list of words you commonly use in your own area of study. Then create an abbreviation for each, and add them to your log.

Vocabulary Power

There are a number of terms and phrases in this lecture that you may encounter in other academic settings. Add at least five vocabulary items to your vocabulary notebook or log.

Match the words in bold from the lecture on the left with a definition on the right.

1. _____ Yesterday we talked about what buildings look like from the outside and what we find **appealing** visually.

2. _____ Today I want to talk about some concerns an architect or engineer has to think about during the construction of a building and also discuss two **approaches** to constructing a building.

3. _____ Many people want to know what **impact** the building will have on the environment.

4. _____ You could **abbreviate** this as D-B-B.

5. _____ It is his or her job to design, determine the **specifications**, produce drawings, hire the best contractors or builders, and manage the entire process from beginning to end.

6. _____ This new approach is less risky because rather than designing everything and then building and hoping for the best, the design and building phases **overlap**.

7. _____ Think on a small **scale** for a minute.

8. _____ Today, architects or engineers need to understand the theory of structures and know how they will **endure** through time.

a. size

b. exact details

c. methods

d. continue

e. shorten

f. attractive

g. repeat

h. effect

Listening 3: Construction and Structural Engineering

Listening to a Lecture

The listening passage is a lecture from an introductory architecture class. The instructor is discussing some things an architect or engineer needs to think about. Throughout the lecture, the instructor uses several time signal words or phrases. Listen two times. The first time, write time signals in your notes using the abbreviations you developed. Make a list of other words you hear that might be good to abbreviate. The second time you listen, take notes on the details on the topic. Use a separate sheet of paper.

Checking Your Understanding: Main Ideas

Review your notes. Listen again to the lecture if necessary, and then put a check mark (✓) next to the statements that best reflect the main ideas.

1. _____ The way buildings look on the outside is the more "fun" part of the construction process.

2. _____ There are two approaches to constructing a building.

3. _____ The environment, planning, and structural theory are three things that need to be considered.

4. _____ The design-build approach is the better choice when constructing a big project.

5. _____ Several characteristics of columns are considered when using them in buildings.

Checking Your Understanding: Details

Use your notes, and put a check mark (✓) next to the best answer. Some questions have more than one answer.

1. When are environmental impact reports important?

   a. _____ in the past

   b. _____ in the present

   c. _____ in the future

2. What types of things are considered during the planning of a building?

   a. _____ materials

   b. _____ location

   c. _____ appearance

3. What are the two approaches to planning?

   a. _____ design-bid-build

   b. _____ design-build

   c. _____ structural theory

   d. _____ environmental impact

4. When did structural theory become important?

   a. _____ in the past

   b. _____ in the present

   c. _____ in the future

5. What factors are considered when determining the building capacity of columns?

   a. _____ dimension

   b. _____ shape

   c. _____ length

   d. _____ material

In-Depth Discussion

Work with a small group. Imagine your architectural firm has been offered the chance to develop a new hotel. Work together, and think about the art and science that is needed for your hotel. Prepare a presentation that addresses the questions.

1. What are the specifications? (how many floors and rooms, length, width?)

   _____

   _____

2. What is the schedule? (how long will it take, when do you expect to complete it)

   _____

   _____

3. What does it look like from the outside?

   _____

   _____

4. What materials are required for construction?

   _____

   _____

5. Where is it located?

   _____

6. How much will it cost? (budget considerations)

   _____

   _____

7. What are some of the challenges you expect during construction?

   _____

   _____

8. Does it serve any other functions other than housing (restaurants, gyms, apartments, shopping)?

   _____

   _____

9. What is the name of the hotel?

   _____

Rapid Vocabulary Review

From the three answers on the right, circle the one that best explains, is an example of, or combines with the vocabulary item on the left as it is used in this unit.

Vocabulary	Answers		
Synonyms			
1. comprising	creating	including	choosing
2. icon	symbol	fame	building
3. span	width	height	length
4. contrasts	differs	resembles	mirrors
5. minor	large	medium	small
6. alterations	changes	plans	designs
7. converted	figured	changed	remained
8. realize	understand	know	learn
9. floors	weights	levels	measurements
10. particular	specific	interesting	different
11. proposed	designed	suggested	constructed
12. required	necessary	important	optional
Combinations and Associations			
13. conflict ___	with	at	around
14. dating ___	to	on	from
15. under ___	threat	fear	alteration
16. become a ___	reality	detail	cue
17. coordinator of a ___	drawing	scale	process
18. hope for ___	the best	a risk	the design
19. figure ___	out	off	under
20. tell me ___	at	with	about

⇨✕⇦ Synthesizing: Projects and Presentations

Short In-Class Speaking Assignments	Longer Outside Assignments
My Dream Office/Workspace	**Social Observation Report**
Describe your dream work environment. What kind of job do you have? Where is it located? What is special about your office or workspace? What factors influence the design of the space? Share your ideas with a small group.	Choose a place where a lot of students spend time. Sit in a place where you can observe different greetings and responses. Take notes on what you hear. Prepare a report that, discusses the similarities and differences that you noticed.
Giving Encouragement	**Interesting Structure Reports**
Your instructor will set a timer for five minutes. Be prepared to state your field of study and talk about why you like it. If you haven't chosen a field yet, choose one that you are interested in. Express opinions. As you are talking, other students will use language to encourage the discussion.	Choose a skyscraper, bridge, tower, or landmark you would like to learn more about. Prepare a presentation about your choice. Include information about its architect, specifications (height, length, or other measurements), materials, location, budget, and schedule (how long it took to build). Give a short presentation to your classmates with the details. Include the goal of the structure, an estimate about how many people use it today, and some other interesting facts.

Vocabulary Log

To increase your vocabulary knowledge, write a definition or translation for each vocabulary item. Then write an original phrase, sentence, or note that will help you remember the vocabulary item.

Vocabulary Item	Definition or Translation	Your Original Phrase, Sentence, or Note
1. produce (v.)	make, create	This factory produces candy.
2. actual		
3. durable		
4. overall		
5. categorized		
6. natural		
7. capacity		
8. element		
9. utility		
10. favorite		
11. fulfill		
12. principles		
13. standard		

Vocabulary Item	Definition or Translation	Your Original Phrase, Sentence, or Note
14. visually		
15. applied		
16. construct (v.)		
17. aspects		
18. blend		
19. collections (n.)		
20. achievements		
21. comprehensive		
22. sector		
23. diverse		
24. agreements (n.)		
25. sites		

2 Marketing: Product Management

Marketing is an important part of business. It involves many disciplines, including psychology, sociology, mathematics, and other business areas. Marketing helps companies decide which products or services are important to people and how to make them interesting to their customers. The marketing process is important not only to make sure customers are happy, but also to ensure that the company makes money from sales.

Part 1: Branding

Pre-Listening Activities

A brand is a symbol, a name, a color, or a slogan for a company, product, or service. Most companies want their brand to be famous and recognized around the world so that customers who see or hear the brand will associate it with a company's products, services, or even its personality. Answer these questions with a partner.

1. What are your favorite brands?

_____

_____

_____

2. "Just Do It" is a slogan that Nike has used. What other slogans can you think of?

_____

_____

_____

3. List some companies or businesses you recognize from their brands.

_____

_____

_____

Strategy: Listening for and Giving Advice

In English, it is important to listen to the speaker, when he or she is giving you advice. There are several ways speakers will give advice. You need to listen carefully and think about who is talking and what the content is to make sure you realize when the person is giving advice and when the person is actually telling you to do something.

Listening for Advice (in approximate order of strength)

You had better
I recommend
Maybe you should
You might want to
You have to
You have to be careful that
If I were you
I would
You might want to (wanna)
Why don't you
You could
It seems to me
How about if you

Listening for the Negative (in approximate order of strength)

I don't think you should
I wouldn't
You shouldn't
You don't have to
You don't need/want to
You wouldn't want to

Pronunciation Note: Intonation is very important. Although advice is worded as suggestions or recommendations, it is really a command or order. In such cases, each word is stressed and the statement has falling intonation. When you do not want to sound too forceful, do not stress each word evenly, think about your tone, and use one of the less formal phrases before your actual advice.

Command: You should study every night.

Less Forceful: If I were you, I would study every night.

Reading

Read some business advice that the South Carolina office of the U.S. Small Business Administration offered to people starting a new business.

Business Basics

(1) "Try to remember how it was when you first started your business," says John LaFond of the SCORE Midlands chapter. "Get back to that survivor mentality."

(2) "Consider closing earlier on slower days," says the Clemson Small Business Development Center.

(3) "Hold your office meeting very early in the day," says the Grand Strand chapter of SCORE. "Keep the meetings short and focused on important issues."

(4) "Streamline your business and become more efficient," says national SCORE, Counselors to America's Small Business. "Use a handheld organizer to keep track of phone numbers, dates, appointments, and meetings. Set a time each week to handle routine tasks, bills, and paperwork."

(5) Create a Board of Advisers, which can be a good source of advice and additional knowledge.

(6) "Look before you leap," says Scott Bellows of the USC Small Business Development Center. Before you make any significant decisions, bounce your plans off of someone else. There's a reason that many companies have a Board of Directors or an Advisory Board. Even a trusted business associate can keep you from digging yourself into a hole that you can't get out of."

(7) "Give up the *toys* like company cars," says John LaFond. (Bonus advice for businesses that depend on car travel: "Get an account with a car rental service instead," Mr. LaFond suggests. You might end up saving money.)

(8) Think tactically: Focus on the next three to six months.

(9) Recognize that "you and your business are two separate financial entities," says Bernell King Ingram of the South Carolina Women's Business Center. "Plan for the financial needs of your business and ALWAYS keep the money separate. Your business gets paid first."

(10) Of course, says the Clemson Small Business Development Center, "Ensure timely filing of government paperwork to avoid fines and penalties."

(11) "Have a business survival plan," says Sandy Davidson of the USC Small Business Development Center in Charleston. "Look for trends and make adjustments accordingly. Have a plan B if undercapitalization surfaces. Know how long you can ride out the storm and when you need to implement plan B."

(12) And finally, "Cut cost," says Bernell King Ingram. Here are some of her suggestions:

1. Meals and entertainment—Have coffee with clients/prospects instead of lunch or dinner.

2. Travel alternatives—Use internet-based meeting and conferencing services if possible.

3. Professional services—Ensure you are getting the best service at the best price (for services like accounting, Web hosting, etc.). Fees vary widely with such services and small businesses often overpay. Negotiate fees; switch services if necessary.

4. Utilities—Do you really need all those perks on your phone line? Also, employ energy-saving techniques and equipment.

Adapted from U.S. Small Business Administration, *Your Local SBA*, "Business Basics."

Listening for and Giving Advice

Work with a partner. Imagine you are a marketing consultant discussing business strategies with someone starting a new business. Give advice from the reading to the other members of your group. Decide which pieces of advice are most important. Choose a phrase that you think is best, and use the tone you think best fits the advice. Take turns being the consultant and the new business owner. Use the space to rewrite the pieces of advice. An example has been done for you.

You might want to get back to that survivor mentality.

_____

_____

_____

_____

_____

_____

_____

_____

_____

_____

_____

_____

_____

_____

Listening 1: Listening for Advice

Listening for Information

The listening passage is a conversation between a student and a professor. They are discussing the student's performance in class. The student wants advice about how to get a better grade. As you listen to the conversation, write answers to the questions.

Listening for Information

1. What advice does the instructor offer?

   _____

   _____

2. What negative advice wording is used?

   _____

   _____

3. Which pieces of advice are stronger? How can you tell?

   _____

   _____

4. Which pieces of advice do you think the student should follow?

   _____

   _____

Speaking

Asking for Advice

Sometimes you want to get advice from someone else. There are some formal and informal ways to ask, depending on the person and situation.

ASKING FOR ADVICE

Formal	Informal
What would you recommend?	What should I do?
What do you suggest?	Any ideas?
Do you think this is okay?	What do you think? Do you have any ideas?
What do you think I should do?	I was wondering, should I [do something]?

Asking for Advice

Think about how you would ask for advice using the phrases in the boxes. Answer the questions. Then share your ideas with the class.

1. How would you ask for advice about each of the situations?

   a. a good restaurant for a formal dinner _____

   b. which computer to buy _____

   c. how to do develop better study habits _____

   d. changing your major _____

   e. the best way to cook chicken _____

   f. ways to save money _____

   g. ways to lose weight _____

2. Who would you ask for advice from each of the situations from Question 1 on page 39?

a. _____   e. _____

b. _____   f. _____

c. _____   g. _____

d. _____

3. What words do you use to ask for advice? To give advice? Add other phrases to the lists on page 39.

_____

_____

4. What things affect the advice and/or the response? Does the place or time of the interaction matter? Does the formality of the question affect the response?

_____

_____

_____

 ## Making Contact

Ask three English speakers for advice about where to take your friends or family when they visit. Take notes on the advice wording you used, the response you received, and the details of the interaction (person's status, age, and gender, the time of day, and the location). Be prepared to discuss your data with the class.

Your Advice Wording	The Person's Response	Details of the Interaction

Part 2: Product Differentiation

Pre-Listening Activities

Think about the variety that exists for each type of product. For example, there is more than one type of mobile phone, soft drink, or brand of jeans. Product differentiation is what marketing professionals do to make their product different from others. This list of differences is what a product needs for consumers to think that product is worth having because it is different from others. Answer these questions with a partner.

1. What brand of mobile phone do you have? What is your favorite soft drink? What brand of jeans do you prefer?

   _____

   _____

   _____

2. Think about two different mobile phones, soft drinks, and jeans. What makes the two different from each other?

   _____

   _____

   _____

3. What do you think are some differences that marketing professionals use to make their products stand out?

   _____

   _____

   _____

Strategy: Listening for and Making Comparisons

In English, speakers use different words and phrases to compare two things. These words are signals to let you know when the speaker wants you to notice the similarities between two different things.

Comparing

also

and

as [big] as

as much as

both . . . and

compared to

either

just as

like

similar/similarly

the same as

the same thing

too

The consumers took a taste test and said the first soft drink tasted the same as the second soft drink.

The marketing manager had to prove that his new product could be compared to the competing product.

The two car brands were similar in both size and price.

Pronunciation Note: Stressing the comparison word or phrase or pausing before and after a word or phrase will indicate to the listener that the speaker thinks the comparison is important.

I would buy EITHER the sweatshirt from the bookstore or the one from the department store.

The original fast food restaurant served hamburgers and fries [pause]; similarly [pause] the new restaurant in town serves those items.

Listening for and Talking about Comparisons

Work with a partner. List five things you have in common. Then write sentences using signal words or phrases from the box on page 42. Share your comparisons with the class.

List

_____

_____

_____

_____

_____

Your Sentences

_____

_____

_____

_____

_____

_____

_____

_____

_____

_____

_____

Speaking

Stating Contrasts

In English, speakers sometimes compare and contrast at the same time. There are certain words or phrases that you can use when you are going to point out a difference to someone. Sometimes you do this after someone has given a similarity or positive idea and you need to state a difference or the negative idea. There are certain words or phrases you can use to contrast two things. Those phrases can be at the beginning or in the middle of the statement.

Contrast Words and Phrases
alternatively
although
as opposed to
but
contrasts with
conversely
despite
even though
however
is different from/than
is the opposite of
on the other hand
or
rather
whereas
while
yet

Stating Contrasts

Work with a partner. List five things you do not have in common. Then write sentences using signal words or phrases from page 44. Share your contrasts with the class.

List

_____

_____

_____

_____

_____

Your Sentences

_____

_____

_____

_____

_____

_____

_____

_____

_____

_____

_____

Listening 2: Comparing and Contrasting

Listening in Pairs (Video)

Listen to the pair of students work together to decide how to prepare for a class project. Discuss the questions in a small group.

Focus on Language

1. What words or phrases giving and asking for advice do the students use?
   <u>Note</u>: Don't worry about writing exact words. Refer to the box on page 34.

   _____

   _____

2. What are some comparisons the students make? What words do they use?
   <u>Note</u>: Don't worry about writing exact words.

   _____

   _____

3. What are some contrasts the students make? What words do they use? <u>Note</u>:
   Don't worry about writing exact words.

   _____

   _____

4. Write any phrases or idioms that you are not familiar with. Discuss what
   they mean and in what type of interactions they are appropriate.

   _____

   _____

Focus on Tone

1. Describe the stress patterns each person uses. Is it clear when comparisons and contrasts are being made?

   _____

   _____

2. How can you tell how each person is feeling about the discussion? Describe the intonation used by each student.

   _____

   _____

3. Is each person's tone appropriate? Why or why not?

   _____

   _____

Focus on Nonverbal Communication

1. What nonverbal cues are used to show how each student feels about ideas from other person?

   _____

   _____

2. Were any of these inappropriate? Why or why not?

   _____

   _____

3. Which student do you think has the most expressive nonverbal communication? Is this good or bad for the interaction?

   _____

   _____

Summary

1. The students agree to focus on the free-range aspect of Sara's in their presentation. Do you agree with them? Why or why not?

   _____

   _____

   _____

   _____

2. Which student uses the best combination of words, tone, and nonverbal communication? Support your answer.

   _____

   _____

   _____

   _____

3. Who would you most want to work with? Why? Who would you rather not work with? Why?

   _____

   _____

   _____

   _____

Ranking

What qualities do you think a film needs to have to make the most money? How can marketing professionals differentiate their movies from others?

Work with a group and list three qualities of films. Then rank them in what you consider the most important difference to the least important.

Our Qualities of Differentiation

_____

_____

_____

_____

Compare and contrast what you know about the top ten highest grossing films world-wide in 2010. Based on your qualities, rank them in order, starting with the ones that made the most money.

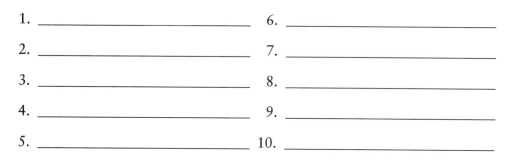

Alice in Wonderland   *Inception*

Clash of the Titans   *Iron Man 2*

Despicable Me   *Shrek Forever After*

Harry Potter and the Death Hallows, Part 1   *Toy Story 3*

The Twilight Saga: Eclipse

How to Train a Dragon

Our Ranking

1. _____   6. _____

2. _____   7. _____

3. _____   8. _____

4. _____   9. _____

5. _____   10. _____

*Information gathered from "2010 Worldwide Grosses" at Box Office Mojo, an IMDb company.

Part 3: Marketing Mix

Pre-Listening Activities

Advertising is a big business. The purpose of advertising is to convince people to use a product. People see advertising everyday in a variety of forms. Some advertisements are directed to a particular group of people; others are placed where the largest number of people can see them. A lot of thought goes into the kinds of advertising used for certain products. Answer these questions with a partner.

1. What is your favorite advertisement? Why do you like it?

   _____

   _____

   _____

2. Other than television commercials, what kinds of advertising can you think of?

   _____

   _____

   _____

3. What are some factors that marketing professionals consider when planning advertising?

   _____

   _____

   _____

Strategy: Listening for and Using Continuation Signal Words and Phrases

Speakers often use signal words and phrases to let you know when they are **continuing** a main idea or theme. These words let you know more ideas or details are coming. Noticing these words and phrases will help you put your notes in study charts and help keep you organized.

Continuation Signal Words and Phrases

additionally

again

another

following

furthermore

in addition

more

moreover

next

therefore

with

Quality and quantity are factors in advertising. **Additionally,** availability should be considered.

Another thing marketing managers think about is where to place the advertisements.

The **next** thing to consider is how the two products are different.

Furthermore, the similarities of products are considered.

Following an analysis of the differences and similarities, the **next** step of a marketing plan can be developed.

What others can you think of to add to the list?

Using Continuation Signal Words and Phrases

Read the sentences in the left column. For each, choose the detail in the right column that is a continuation of the main idea.

1. _____ Advertising is a popular job.

2. _____ People who get a degree in marketing will have an easier time finding an advertising job.

3. _____ Marketing managers sometimes have to travel a lot.

4. _____ Marketing managers develop strategies to make the company money.

5. _____ Marketing managers work with researchers and product development managers.

a. They may have to work long hours and on weekends.

b. They work with high-level managers.

c. Those with creativity skills and previous work experience get the best jobs.

d. Competition for positions is high.

e. They make sure the company's customers are happy.

What words would you use to connect each one? Write a sentence (or two) connecting the ideas using a continuation signal word or phrase from the box on page 51. Note that some rewording may be necessary depending on which continuation signal word or phrase you choose.

1. _____

_____

2. _____

_____

3. _____

_____

4. _____

_____

5. _____

_____

✏ Note-Taking

Strategy: Using a T-Chart

A T-chart is a graphic organizer that you can use while you are taking notes or to organize your notes later. A T-chart is helpful when comparing and contrasting two things, evaluating the advantages or disadvantages, or examining the strengths and weaknesses. They are also helpful when listing facts and opinions or main ideas and details.

Sample T-chart headings may be Similarities and Differences, Advantages and Disadvantages, or Main Ideas and Details. A sample T-chart may look like this.

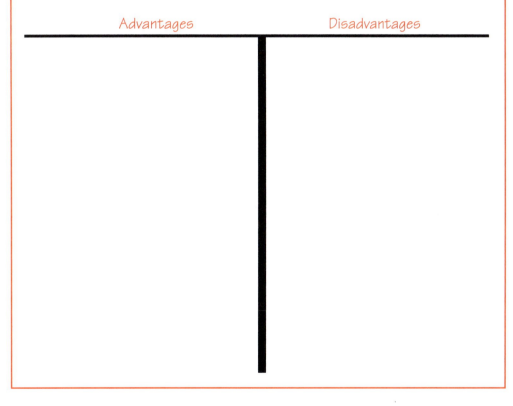

Advantages   Disadvantages

Developing a T-Chart

Work with a partner, and think of a product that you both use but where you each use different brands, such as toothpaste, shampoo, or soap. Write the brand names above your T-chart. Then list similarities and differences in the columns.

Vocabulary Power

There are a number of terms and phrases in this lecture that you may encounter in other academic settings. Add at least five vocabulary items to your vocabulary notebook or log.

Match the words in bold from the lecture on the left with a definition on the right.

1. _____ Some are very **obvious,** such as commercials on television or advertisements on the radio.

2. _____ Perhaps you've gotten a **stack** of coupons in the mail or you see a flyer for a new product posted on campus.

3. _____ In fact, it's been around since 1960 and has been **widely** accepted thanks to a well-known marketer, E. Jerome McCarthy.

4. _____ You'll see this **concept** well documented in your textbook and most marketing textbooks in print.

5. _____ The product is the actual **item** you're trying to sell.

6. _____ **Rather,** this is the place where the product can be bought by the consumer.

7. _____ My last main point for today is about **covert** advertising. This is the advertising that people may not even realize is advertising.

8. _____ Sometimes actors will **mention** a specific brand or they'll be using a computer and you can clearly see what kind of computer it is.

a. in many locations

b. idea

c. say

d. clear; easy to see

e. hidden; not seen; not obvious

f. pile; group

g. instead

h. thing

Listening 3: The Marketing Mix

Listening to a Lecture

The listening passage is a lecture from an introductory marketing class. The instructor is explaining the parts of the marketing mix and some different types of advertising. The lecturer gives main ideas and details. As you listen, take notes. Then, try to organize your notes into a T-chart with the headings *Main Ideas* and *Details*. Use a separate sheet of paper.

Checking Your Understanding: Main Ideas

Review your notes and T-chart. Listen again to the lecture if necessary, and then put a check mark (✔) next to the statements that best reflect the main ideas.

1. _____ There are four parts to the marketing mix.

2. _____ The marketing mix is well documented in textbooks.

3. _____ Place and location near where advertising is used.

4. _____ Advertising includes paid communication.

5. _____ Covert advertising is communication we don't realize is advertising.

Checking Your Understanding: Details

Use your notes and T-chart, put a check mark (✓) next to the best answer. Some questions have more than one answer.

1. What are the four Ps in the marketing mix?

    a. _____ pop-up box

    b. _____ product

    c. _____ price

    d. _____ place

    e. _____ phone order

    f. _____ promotion

2. What specific types of advertising does the instructor discuss?

    a. _____ television commercials

    b. _____ phone orders

    c. _____ sponsorships

    d. _____ public relations

3. Where can you find examples of covert advertising?

    a. _____ billboards

    b. _____ signs on buses

    c. _____ video games

    d. _____ movies

4. What are examples of "place"?

    a. _____ television advertisements

    b. _____ physical stores

    c. _____ infomercial

    d. _____ website

In-Depth Discussion

Work with a small group. Imagine your marketing team has been offered the chance to advertise a new electronic game. Work together, and think about the product and the advertising plan. Prepare a presentation that addresses these questions.

1. What is the name of the game? Describe it.

   _____

   _____

2. Who do you expect to buy the game?

   _____

   _____

3. How is it packaged?

   _____

   _____

4. How much does it cost?

   _____

   _____

5. What is the branding (symbol, slogan, etc.)?

   _____

   _____

6. Where will you advertise (magazines, television, etc.)? Why are these the best places?

   _____

   _____

7. What percentage of your budget will you spend on each type of advertising?

   _____

   _____

8. Will you participate in any covert advertising? Give examples.

   _____

   _____

Rapid Vocabulary Review

From the three answers on the right, circle the one that best explains, is an example of, or combines with the vocabulary item on the left as it is used in this unit.

Vocabulary	Answers		
Synonyms			
1. encounter	find	hurt	love
2. a task	a small feeling	a small job	a small mistake
3. whereas	and	but	or
4. vary	be correct	be different	be early
5. a billboard	advertising	paying	weakness
6. appropriate	low	opinion	suitable
7. such as	for example	right now	take care
8. tips	illnesses	machines	suggestions
9. furthermore	additionally	completely	potentially
10. switch	believe	change	decrease
11. a strategy	a bill	a joke	a plan
12. a fine	you buy it	you make it	you pay it
Combinations and Associations			
13. make ___	sure	thought	weather
14. ride out the ___	wave	snow	storm
15. on the other ___	foot	hand	eye
16. high-level ___	dollars	managers	pets
17. as much ___	over	in	as
18. ___ advice	can	give	home
19. a slogan ___	for an animal	for a company	for a friend
20. focus ___	at	on	until

⇨✗⇦ Synthesizing: Projects and Presentations

Short In-Class Speaking Assignments	Longer Outside Assignments
Compare and Contrast	**How Should We Advise This Person?**
Line up so that half the class faces the other half of the class. For one minute, talk with the person across from you. Make statements comparing and contrasting what each of you is wearing. After one minute, move to the right and compare/contrast with the next person.	Look at the local newspapers or online for the advice columns. Choose a letter asking for advice that you think is interesting. Do not show the answer to anyone yet. Pass the letter around the class. Collect advice from others in the class on the same piece of paper. Then read your letter, all the advice, and then the advice the "expert" from the newspaper gave. Prepare a short presentation for your classmates.
Differentiation	**Powerful Advertising**
Review T-chart on page 53. Work with a partner, and list your favorite movies. Then compare/contrast them. Create a T-chart and present that to the rest of the class.	Bring in an advertisement from a magazine or a video clip of a television commercial. Share the advertisement with a small group, and then discuss the four Ps: product, price, place, and promotion. Talk about what you would do in the same way and what you would do differently if you were on the marketing team for that product.

Vocabulary Log

To increase your vocabulary knowledge, write a definition or translation for each vocabulary item. Then write an original phrase, sentence, or note that will help you remember the vocabulary item.

Vocabulary Item	Definition or Translation	Your Original Phrase, Sentence, or Note
1. gross	to make (money)	That movie grossed 100 million dollars.
2. a factor		
3. a fee		
4. at least		
5. furthermore		
6. involve		
7. covert		
8. plan B		
9. competition		
10. implement (v.)		
11. an infomercial		
12. a meal		
13. take turns		

Vocabulary Item	Definition or Translation	Your Original Phrase, Sentence, or Note
14. streamline (v.)		
15. an appointment		
16. advice		
17. widely		
18. leap		
19. a client		
20. a slogan		
21. additional		
22. end up		
23. a penalty		
24. associate		
25. file (v.)		

3 Earth Science: Earth's Composition

Earth science is a general term for all the sciences that study the planet. Earth scientists study the land, but they also study the oceans and atmosphere. They use parts of other sciences, such as chemistry or biology, and other disciplines, such as math, to study how Earth works and why it looks the way it does. This unit explores Earth's structure and composition, the tools used to study it, and phenomena affecting it.

Part 1: Global Positioning

Pre-Listening Activities

The planet has been studied for centuries. **Geodesy** is an earth science that measures the size and shape of the planet. Although this branch of science has existed for a long time, it has changed with inventions in technology. This branch of earth science gives an address to every point on Earth and makes global positioning possible. Answer these questions with a partner.

1. Have you ever used a global positioning system (GPS)? Where were you? Why did you choose to use it?

   _____

   _____

   _____

2. Do you have a global positing system (GPS) in your car or on your phone? What are the advantages of having a GPS?

   _____

   _____

   _____

3. How do you think geodesy has changed? How has it stayed the same?

   _____

   _____

   _____

Strategy: Listening for and Giving Interesting Facts

Speakers will use certain words or phrases when giving information that they think is especially interesting. The facts might be surprising, unusual, funny, new, or simply something interesting. If the speaker thinks it is interesting, it is probably something you should note. Remember that you may not find it as interesting as the speaker, but because he or she is stressing it, you need to make a note. In these cases, there are certain words and phrases to listen for.

Giving Interesting Facts

As a matter of fact

As funny as it sounds

Interestingly/Interestingly enough

Believe it or not

Funny thing

The thing is

Oddly

Surprisingly/Surprising

This sounds [strange].

Strange/Strangely

What I find most [interesting] is _____.

Interestingly enough, no one really knows when the debate started.

Oddly, the test did not show the results they expected.

As funny as this sounds, I really want to study on Friday night.

Pronunciation Note: Phrases that precede interesting facts are usually followed by a pause. Then, the content word that is interesting, new, surprising, or unusual is stressed so the listener knows what is most important.

Believe it or not, [pause] the **biggest** earthquake in 2010 was not the **deadliest.**

Reading

Read some information about geodesy (pronunciation: jee-ah-des-ee) and how it is used today.

What Is Geodesy?

(1) Geodesy, is the science of measuring and monitoring the size and shape of the Earth. Geodesists give addresses to points all over the Earth. If you were to stick pins in a model of the Earth and then give each of those pins an address, then you would be doing what a geodesist does. By looking at the height, angles, and distances between these locations, geodesists create a spatial reference system that everyone can use.

(2) Geologists, oceanographers, meteorologists, and even paleontologists use geodesy to understand physical processes on, above, and within the Earth. Because geodesy makes extremely accurate measurements (to the centimeter level), scientists can use its results to determine exactly how much the Earth's surface has changed over very short and very long periods of time (*Careers in Geodesy,* 1986).

(3) The Earth's surface changes for many reasons. For instance, its surface rises and falls about 30 centimeters (about 1 foot) every day due to the gravitational influences of the moon and the sun. The Earth's outermost layer, the crust, is made up of a dozen or more "plates" that ride atop a sea of molten rock, called magma, which flows beneath the surface of the Earth.

(4) Plate tectonics is the scientific discipline that looks at how these plates shift and interact, especially in relation to earthquakes and volcanoes. Although these phenomena are violent and usually affect large areas of land, even smaller events, such as erosion and storms, have an impact on shaping the Earth's surface. Geodesy helps us determine exactly where and how much the Earth's surface is changing.

(5) Building roads and bridges, performing land surveys, and making maps are some of the important activities that depend on a spatial reference system. Spatial reference systems can locate any spot on Earth quickly and accurately. Speed and accuracy are important. For example, if you build a bridge, you need to know where to start on both sides of the river. If you don't, your bridge may not meet in the middle.

(6) As positioning and navigation have become fundamental to the functions of society, geodesy has become more important. It helps the transportation industry be safe and reliable and save money. Without geodesy, planes might land next to—rather than at—airports, and ships could crash onto land. Geodesy also helps shipping companies save time and money by shortening their ships' and airplanes' routes and lowering the amount of fuel they use.

Adapted from U.S. Department of Commerce, National Oceanic and Atmospheric Administration, *NOAA Ocean Service Education*, "What is Geodesy."

Drawing Attention to Interesting Facts

Use the reading to answer these questions.

1. If you were giving this information in a lecture, which sentences would you start with a phrase indicating you think it is especially interesting, surprising, or unusual information?

   _____

   _____

   _____

   _____

2. Why did you choose the sentences you did?

   _____

   _____

3. Rewrite two sentences and read them to a partner. Did you choose the same sentences? Did you choose the same phrases? Were are able to stress the interesting, surprising, or unusual content words?

   _____

   _____

   _____

   _____

   _____

   _____

Listening 1: Listening for Interesting Facts

Listening for Information

This listening passage is a conversation between a student and a teaching assistant. They are discussing the national spatial reference system. The student wants more information about the content to determine the topic of his research paper. As you listen to the conversation, write answers to the questions.

1. What phrases does the teaching assistant use to indicate which facts she finds most interesting?

   _____

   _____

2. Which points does the teaching assistant find most interesting?

   _____

   _____

3. How does the student encourage conversation? Review the box on pages 3–4.

   _____

   _____

4. Which fact do you think the student should research?

   _____

   _____

Speaking

Using the Telephone

There are three steps to beginning most phone calls.

Step 1: Open with a greeting.

Step 2: Identify yourself.

You should give your name or let the person know where they know you from. Depending on who you are calling, you may also have to ask for a person or a department. Once you reach the person you are calling, you should complete step three.

Step 3: State the purpose of your call.

There are several ways to state the purpose of your call. Starting your reason with a purpose phrase will alert your listener that you're about to say exactly what you need.

USING THE TELEPHONE

Identifying Yourself	Stating Your Purpose
My name is [Charles Timson].	I'm calling to ask about [the test].
This is [Darrin Michaels].	I need to find out [when your office hours are].
This is [Nathan Williams], and I am a student in your English class.	I was wondering if you could explain [how to get to your office].
I'm taking your Earth Science 101 class.	I wanted to ask if [the bookstore had any special prices this week].
This is [Lucy], and I'm in your morning class.	I'm hoping to learn [when tickets will be on sale].
I'm [Tim], and my roommate is in your earth science class.	I'm interested in buying [a DVD]. Could you tell me how much [the DVD costs]?

Using the Telephone

Think about using the telephone, and then answer these questions with a partner.

1. What would you say in each situation?

    a. you dialed the wrong number _____

    _____

    b. you need to be transferred to another department _____

    _____

    c. your friend's roommate answers the phone _____

    _____

    d. your instructor's husband answers the phone _____

    _____

    e. you want to file a complaint with the phone company _____

    _____

    f. you need to make a doctor's appointment _____

    _____

    g. you have to get the homework assignment from the instructor _____

    _____

2. What things affect the phrasing you choose? Does the place or time of the interaction matter? Does it matter who you are calling?

    _____

    _____

3. Under what circumstances is it better to call an instructor rather than send an email message?

    _____

    _____

Making Contact

Make two phone calls to get answers to the questions listed in the chart from your school or from a local college or university. Take notes on the response you received and the details of the interaction (person's status, age, and gender, the time of day, and the location). Be prepared to discuss your data with the class.

Office	Question	The Person's Response	Details of the Interaction
Registrar	How much does a transcript cost?		
Athletics	What grade point average is required for student athletes?		
Financial Aid	What is the deadline for financial aid applications?		
Campus Safety	How much does a campus parking ticket cost?		
Transportation	Where is your office located?		
Admissions	What TOEFL® score is required for admission?		
Your Department	Who is teaching _____ next term?		

Part 2: Earthquakes

Pre-Listening Activities

Part 1 explored mapping the earth's surface. Part 2 addresses a natural phenomenon that has affected earth's surface: earthquakes. An earthquake causes the Earth's crust to shake or roll. It is the Earth's way of releasing stress, but it can change the way things look. Earthquakes not only can alter manmade constructions, but they also alter the earth itself. Answer these questions with a partner.

1. Have you ever felt an earthquake? Where were you? What was it like?

   _____

   _____

   _____

2. What areas do you know of that are likely to have earthquakes? Would you want to live there?

_____

_____

_____

3. What is the biggest earthquake that you are familiar with? What sort of damage did it do? Did it change the Earth's surface?

_____

_____

_____

_____

_____

_____

Strategy: Listening for and Using Questions to Check for Comprehension

Sometimes when people are giving a lot of information, such as during a lecture, or when they can't judge your understanding face-to-face, such as on the telephone, they will ask a question to make sure you understood or got all the information you needed. This is called **checking for comprehension.** Deciding when to check for comprehension may depend on the vocabulary, the amount of information, how much the audience already knows about the topic, or some other factor. The speaker decides when to ask. Make sure to notice when speakers use these checks. They are probably asking after they give information they think is important. There are formal and informal ways to do this.

Formal Questions

Do you understand?

Are you following me?

Is that clear?

Do you see what I mean?/See what I mean?

Does that make sense?

Know what I mean?

See what I'm saying?

Informal Questions

Got it?

Are you with me?

Make sense?

Okay?

You know?

Pronunciation Note: Questions that are intended to check comprehension are usually asked because someone really wants an answer. Therefore, when asking one, remember to pause after the question to give people a time to

Using Questions to Check for Comprehension

Think about situations where checking for comprehension is important, and answer these questions with a partner.

1. Which of these people do you think should use a more formal questions to check for comprehension? Why?

    a. a professor _____

    b. a roommate _____

    c. a group of classmates _____

    d. friends _____

    e. parents talking to young children _____

    f. adults talking with their parents _____

    g. customer service representatives taking calls for a company _____

2. What other questions that check for comprehension have you heard? Can you add any others to the list?

    _____

    _____

3. What settings or topics do you think affect the formality or need for a question to check for comprehension? List as many as you can.

    _____

    _____

Speaking

Stating Comprehension or Incomprehension

When people check for your understanding, you should let them know if you understand or if you caught everything they said. If you don't, be honest. This is a good time to let them know that you don't understand everything or that you missed a piece of information. You can let the other people know about your comprehension even if they don't ask first. Some common phrases to do this are listed.

Comprehension	Incomprehension
I understand.	I'm not sure I understand.
I know what you mean.	Can you say that again?
I get it.	I'm sorry.
Got it.	I don't get it.
Makes sense.	What was that?
I'm good./I'm OK.	Huh?

Checking for and Stating Comprehension

Work with a small group. Choose a box of facts to write about on a separate sheet of paper. Imagine you are the instructor lecturing students about the 1906 San Francisco earthquake. Write sentences based on the facts you have to give to the other members of your group. Check for their comprehension when it is appropriate. Be prepared for them to state their comprehension or incomprehension during your lecture. Take turns being the instructor and the student.

Box A

Happened April 18, 1906

One of the most significant earthquakes

Fault rupture was 296 miles along the San Andreas fault

Confused geologists because they didn't have knowledge of plate tectonics

A professor named Reid analyzed the crust and created his elastic-rebound theory of the earthquake source (still the main model of the earthquake cycle today)

Box B

Started with a foreshock at 5:12 AM with the actual quake starting 20–25 seconds later

Epicenter was near San Francisco, but it was felt in Oregon and Nevada

Shaking lasted 45–60 seconds

The highest Modified Mercalli Intensities (MMIs) were from VII to IX

The MMIs were parallel to the length of the rupture and were as long as 80 kilometers

---

Box C

A professor named Lawson noticed the intensity and geologic conditions were linked

Areas with sediment had stronger shaking than areas with bedrock

Earthquake is most remembered for the fire it started

The earthquake and fire caused over 700 deaths, but the exact number is not certain

Most deaths were in San Francisco, but 189 were reported in other places

---

Data from *U.S. Geological Survey,* "The Great 1906 San Francisco Earthquake, http://earthquake.usgs.gov/regional/nca/1906/18april/.

Listening 2: Making Sure Everyone Understands

Listening in Groups (Video)

Listen to the students talk with their instructor about an assignment for their earth science class. Discuss the questions in a small group.

Focus on Language

1. Which phrase does the instructor use before talking about a fact she finds interesting? <u>Note</u>: Don't worry about writing exact words. Refer to the box on page 64.

   _____

   _____

2. What examples of checking for comprehension did you hear? <u>Note</u>: Don't worry about writing exact words.

   _____

   _____

3. How do the students state their understanding? <u>Note</u>: Don't worry about writing exact words.

   _____

   _____

   _____

Focus on Tone

1. Do both students really understand the assignment? Support your answers.

   _____

   _____

   _____

2. Does the instructor leave enough time after checking for comprehension?

_____

_____

3. Is each person's tone appropriate? Why or why not?

_____

_____

Focus on Nonverbal Communication

1. What nonverbal cues are used to show how each member of the group feels about the content? Who do you think has the most interest in the assignment?

_____

_____

2. Was any nonverbal communication inappropriate? Why or why not?

_____

_____

3. Which student do you think has the most expressive nonverbal communication? Is this good or bad for the interaction?

_____

_____

Summary

1. Do you think this instructor did a good job of making sure students
   understand? Why or why not?

   _____

   _____

   _____

   _____

2. What do you think is interesting about the assignment? What do you think
   is most interesting about this interaction?

   _____

   _____

   _____

   _____

3. Who would you most want to work with? Why? Who would you rather not
   work with? Why?

   _____

   _____

   _____

   _____

Information Gap

Earthquakes have been taking place around the world for centuries, some long before the Richter Scale existed to measure them. Now, more scientific and detailed records are kept.

Work with a partner to complete the chart of the largest earthquakes from 1996 to March 2011. Person A has Chart 1 on this page, and Person B has Chart 2 on page 82. Work back to back to complete the information. Ask for information and for clarification if you need to.

CHART 1

LARGEST EARTHQUAKES, 1996–MARCH 2011

Year	Date	Magnitude on the Richter Scale	Fatalities	Region
2011	March 11	9.0	28,050	Japan
2010		8.8	507	Chile
2009	September 29		192	Samoa Islands
2008	May 12	7.9		China
2007	September 12		25	Indonesia
2006	November 15	8.3	0	Kuril Islands
2005	March 28	8.6	1,313	
2004	December 26	9.1		Northern Sumatra
2003	September 25		0	Japan
2002	November 3	7.9	0	Alaska
2001	June 23	8.4	138	
2000		8.0	2	Ireland
1999	September 20	7.7	2,297	
1998	March 25	8.1	0	Balleny Islands
1997	October 14, December 5	7.8	0	Fiji Kamchatka
1996		8.2		Indonesia

Data from: *U.S. Geological Service*, "Largest and Deadliest Earthquakes by Year," http://earthquake.usgs.gov/earthquakes/eqarchives/year/byyear.php.

CHART 2

LARGEST EARTHQUAKES, 1996–MARCH 2011

Year	Date	Magnitude on the Richter Scale	Fatalities	Region
2011	March 11	9.0	28,050	Japan
2010	February 27	8.8	507	
2009	September 29	8.1		Samoa Islands
2008	May 12		87,587	China
2007		8.5	25	Indonesia
2006	November 15	8.3	0	
2005	March 26	8.6		Indonesia
2004	December 26		227,898	Northern Sumatra
2003		8.3	0	Japan
2002	November 3	7.9	0	Alaska
2001	June 23	8.4	138	Peru
2000	November 16		2	Ireland
1999	September 20	7.7		Taiwan
1998	March 25	8.1	0	
1997		7.8	0	Fiji Kamchatka
1996	February 17	8.2	166	Indonesia

Data from: *U.S. Geological Service,* "Largest and Deadliest Earthquakes by Year," http://earthquake. usgs.gov/earthquakes/eqarchives/year/byyear.php.

Part 3: Types of Rocks

Pre-Listening Activities

The Earth is made of rock, and there are many types of rocks. Surprisingly, most rocks on the surface are formed from only eight elements. However, those eight elements can be combined in many ways to make rocks look very different. For this reason, many people collect rocks. Answer these questions with a partner.

1. Do you have any collections? What do you collect? Would you ever be interested in collecting rocks?

   _____

   _____

   _____

2. What do think would be interesting about different types of rocks? What would a rock have to look like to be added to your collection?

   _____

   _____

   _____

3. Can you guess how rocks change and what causes those changes?

   _____

   _____

   _____

Strategy: Listening for and Using Classification or Example Signal Words and Phrases

Speakers often use signal words to let you know when they will be giving you examples of things that fall into the same category or classification. It is a good idea to notice these because it helps you organize your notes during and after a lecture. Speakers will use certain words to indicate when material will be divided by category. Then, they'll indicate what material fits into which category and give examples.

Classification (Example) Signal Words and Phrases

- **categories, classes, classifications, divisions, groups, kinds, sections, types**

   Rocks fall into three basic **categories:** igneous, sedimentary, and metamorphic.

   There are three **classes** of rocks, igneous, sedimentary, and metamorphic. Each has many **examples** or **divisions.**

- *for example, for instance, an example, a good example*

   For example, oxygen is an element that often found in rocks.

   Volcanoes produce igneous rocks; **for instance,** pumice.

- *the following*

   The following are examples of common elements in rocks: oxygen, iron, and aluminum.

- *such as*

   Rocks are primarily made from eight elements, **such as** oxygen, iron, and aluminum.

- *specifically*

   Rocks are primarily made from eight elements, **specifically,** oxygen, iron, and aluminum.

- *illustrated by, to illustrate*

   Igneous rocks are made from volcanoes. **To illustrate,** think about basinite, basalt, or pumice.

What others can you think of to add to the list?

Listening for and Using Classification or Example Signal Words and Phrases

Work with a group. Look at the categories listed. Think of three examples to fit into each category. Then write sentences using classification and example signal words or phrases. Present your lists to the other groups.

1. private and public universities

_____

_____

_____

2. science disciplines

_____

_____

_____

3. types of foods

_____

_____

_____

4. best vacation destinations

_____

_____

_____

5. benefits of learning English

_____

_____

_____

Note-Taking

Strategy: Using a Classification Chart

When you realize that the course material is categorized, you can use a classification chart to take notes during the lecture or organize them later. A classification chart is a good way to put similar ideas in the same category or organize examples.

Classification charts are flexible because you can design them the based on the information you have. Sometimes you have more information so you may want long columns. A chart like that might look like this.

Types of Rocks

Type 1: _____	Type 2: _____	Type 3: _____
Information and Examples	Information and Examples	Information and Examples

Other times, it may be helpful to tie the categories to a general category or sub-divide the information. In that case, a classification chart might look like this.

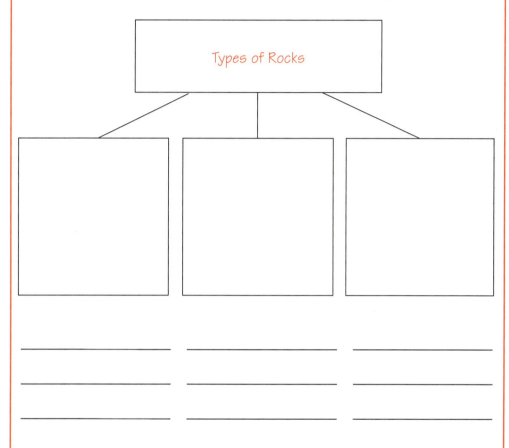

Types of Rocks

You'll have a chance to practice classification and example signal words and taking notes in a chart during the lecture. Thinking about them before will help you use them and miss less of what the instructor is saying.

Creating a Classification Chart

Work with a group. On a separate piece of paper, make a classification chart for one of the items in the activity on page 85. Add information and list your examples. Be prepared to show your classification chart to your classmates.

Vocabulary Power

There are a number of terms and phrases in this lecture that you may encounter in other academic settings. Add at least five vocabulary items to your vocabulary notebook or log.

Match the words in bold from the lecture on the left with a definition on the right.

1. _____ We've been talking about rocks and how they are always in a **state** of change.

    a. not tight; not compact

2. _____ Rocks that you find outside this building might have been formed deep below the crust and only made their way to the **surface** after millions of years.

    b. become liquid

    c. condition

3. _____ Remember, the Earth is **over** four billion years old.

    d. more than

    e. outer part

4. _____ If everyone is ready, let's **dig in.**

    f. exit

5. _____ Igneous rocks are formed by rock that has **melted,** then cooled, and then hardened back into rock.

    g. begin

    h. liquid

6. _____ In some cases, it may then **erupt** from a volcano.

7. _____ Contrasting with igneous again, these are not made of **molten** rock but are made of accumulations of materials, or sediments.

8. _____ Surprisingly, these rocks are actually very **loose**—they barely hold together sometimes.

Listening 3: Types of Rocks

Listening to a Lecture

The listening passage is a lecture from an introductory earth science class. The instructor is discussing the three types of rocks. Throughout the lecture, the instructor gives some information about each type and gives examples. Listen two times. The first time, take notes as you would normally. Then develop a classification chart based on the information. Complete the chart with the information you have. Then listen again, and add more details to your chart.

Checking Your Understanding: Main Ideas

Review your notes. Listen again to the lecture if necessary, and then put a check mark (✓) next to the statements that best reflect the main ideas.

1. _____ Rocks are made up of only eight elements.

2. _____ There are three basic rock types.

3. _____ Eventually, all rocks make it to the surface of the Earth.

4. _____ There are many examples of each type of rock.

5. _____ Rocks are classified by how and where they're formed.

Checking Your Understanding: Details

Use your notes, and put a check mark (✓) next to the best answer. Some questions have more than one answer.

1. What are examples of igneous rocks?

   a. _____ obsidian

   b. _____ granite

   c. _____ jade

   d. _____ coal

   e. _____ basalt

   f. _____ limestone

   g. _____ marble

2. What are characteristic of sedimentary rocks?

   a. _____ They're from volcanoes.

   b. _____ They're sometimes very loose.

   c. _____ They're formed from high pressure.

   d. _____ They're held together by electrical attraction.

3. What are examples of sedimentary rocks?

   a. _____ granite

   b. _____ coal

   c. _____ basalt

   d. _____ slate

   e. _____ limestone

   f. _____ sandstone

4. What is an interesting fact about metamorphic rocks?

   a. _____ They're made of accumulations of other materials.

   b. _____ They're formed at the surface of the crust.

   c. _____ They're formed from one of the other types.

   d. _____ Their form is very loose.

5. Which are examples of metamorphic rocks?

   a. _____ sandstone

   b. _____ limestone

   c. _____ slate

   d. _____ chalk

   e. _____ obsidian

   f. _____ marble

   g. _____ material

In-Depth Discussion

Work with a small group. Imagine you have the chance to take a trip around the world to see what the planet Earth has to offer. Work with your team to create an itinerary of places. You want to create a list of places to visit based on these categories. Try to think of at least two examples for each category.

1. places to see volcanoes _____

_____

2. the places most likely to experience an earthquake _____

_____

3. the best place to see a lot of rocks _____

_____

4. the best place to experience the Earth's oceans _____

_____

5. the best place to see the stars (or into outer space) _____

_____

6. the most dangerous places on the planet _____

_____

7. the best mountains _____

_____

8. the oldest places _____

_____

9. the hottest places _____

_____

10. the coldest places _____

_____

Rapid Vocabulary Review

From the three answers on the right, circle the one that best explains, is an example of, or combines with the vocabulary item on the left as it is used in this unit.

Vocabulary	Answers		
Synonyms			
1. an assignment	dangerous	homework	sleeping
2. location	person	place	thing
3. one sort	one belief	one noise	one type
4. atmosphere	air	birthday	beverage
5. a phrase	group of letters	group of sounds	group of words
6. stick around	stay	poke	try
7. precede	come after	come before	come between
8. the setting of a story	the main idea	the place	the characters
9. routes	cats, dogs	roads, streets	weather, wind
10. likely	agree	probable	really
11. odd	excellent	many	strange
12. fuel	gasoline	people	weather
Combinations and Associations			
13. find out ___	food	information	rain
14. ___ an appointment	do	make	run
15. such ___	as	in	of
16. a complaint about ___	an excellent flight	a great test	a noisy neighbor
17. a branch of a ___	person	chair	tree
18. damage ___	to your breakfast	to your house	to your pencils
19. depend ___	of	on	out
20. a wrong ___	cheese	number	umbrella

⇨⧓⇦ Synthesizing: Projects and Presentations

Short In-Class Speaking Assignments	Longer Outside Assignments
My Field of Study	**My Collection**
Describe your field of study, and talk about it with a small group. If you haven't officially selected one, select one you are interested in. Make sure to insert comprehension check questions and be prepared to explain if you notice that your classmates aren't following the information. Draw their attention to the details you find most interesting.	Prepare a presentation on something you collect. Talk about why you collect this item, where you get your items, and how many items are currently in your collection. Then explain how you classify the items and give examples. Bring some examples or pictures to use as visual aids for your presentation. Include phrases from this unit.
On the Phone	**Lab Report: We Go Together**
Write something that you would like to buy and a type of food you would like to eat on a piece of paper. For example, you may write "I'd like to buy flowers for my friend's birthday" or "I want to try Thai food." Turn in your paper. Your instructor will give you someone else's paper. Find a store or restaurant, and call that business to learn more information. Bring information about the places, locations, prices, or other details you learn from your calls. Be prepared to exchange information.	Find three rocks on campus or near where you live. Do some light research and then work with a partner in class to complete a lab report on your rocks. Include information about where you found each rock, what it looks like (its physical characteristics), what kind of rock you think it is (igneous, sedimentary, or metamorphic), and where you think it came from. It isn't important if you guess incorrectly. Focus on using phrases from this unit and thinking about information that would be needed in a science class. Be prepared to compare and contrast your three rocks with others your classmates bring.

Vocabulary Log

To increase your vocabulary knowledge, write a definition or translation for each vocabulary item. Then write an original phrase, sentence, or note that will help you remember the vocabulary item.

Vocabulary Item	Definition or Translation	Your Original Phrase, Sentence, or Note
1. linked	connected	England and the U.S. are linked by history.
2. state (v.)		
3. however		
4. parallel		
5. flexible		
6. significant		
7. combine		
8. intensity		
9. the magnitude		
10. a geologist		
11. a term		
12. a cue		
13. illustrate		

Vocabulary Item	Definition or Translation	Your Original Phrase, Sentence, or Note
14. a number of		
15. exact		
16. eventually		
17. measure (v.)		
18. a century		
19. be made up of		
20. a destination		
21. accumulation		
22. loose		
23. a category		
24. a benefit		
25. indicate		

4

U.S. History: Presidents

History is a record of the past for any event, people, or place that involved humans. People who study history are called historians, and they record who, what, where, when, and why events took place. This unit will discuss some important people in U.S. history—namely Presidents Lincoln, Kennedy, and Nixon—and how events during their presidencies helped shape the way that the United States is today.

Part 1: Abraham Lincoln

Pre-Listening Activities

Abraham Lincoln was the 16th president of the United States. He served from 1861 to 1865, when he was shot by an actor named John Wilkes Booth. As a young man, he had a variety of different jobs, had a family, and started a law career before entering politics. He is considered by many to have been one of the best U.S. presidents. He is one of the four presidents whose image was carved into rock at Mount Rushmore (see page 96). (Do you know who the other presidents are in the photo on page 96?) Answer these questions with a partner.

1. Have you heard of Abraham Lincoln? What do you already know about him?

   _____

   _____

   _____

2. What qualities or experience does a person need to be a good president?

   _____

   _____

   _____

3. What makes a person a good leader?

   _____

   _____

   _____

Strategy: Listening for and Taking Guesses

Sometimes you may not be sure of the information you are going to share. It's okay to take a guess, but you need to let the listener know that you're not certain. Likewise, when you're listening, you need to recognize when someone is not certain. This affects how you take notes and decide what information is the most important. There are certain phrases that are used before a statement that indicate when someone may be taking a guess or when someone is simply offering an opinion.

Taking a Guess

I'd guess he/she/it is/was

I'd guess that

I'd say he/she/it means

It might be

I think it's [partly] because

It looks/sounds like

Perhaps/Maybe

I'm not sure/don't know, but

It could be [due to]

I'm just guessing that it's/My guess is

I wonder

That might be

Pronunciation Note: English words are not always said separately or clearly. Some words are **linked** or joined with the word after it. For example, words that end in a consonant are linked or joined to a word that begins with a vowel. It sounds like one word instead of two. Therefore, the phrase *I'd guess it's* might sound like *I'dguessit's*.

Why was Lincoln considered a great leader?

I'd guess it's because he had military experience.

I'd say it's because he was a good speaker.

I think it's because he brought an end to slavery.

Listening for and Taking Guesses

Read Lincoln's most famous speech, *The Gettysburg Address*, on page 100. Work with a partner. Divide the reading into two parts.

1. Mark the places where linking between final consonant and beginning vowel sounds could occur. Draw lines or highlight them in the text. Then practice reading the speech and linking the words. Exchange parts, and practice linking the words in the other half of the speech.

2. Choose three sentences from your half of the speech, and take a guess at what Lincoln meant. Begin your statement with an appropriate phrase. You can use one from the box on page 98 or you can adapt one. Read your guesses to your partner.

   a. _____

   _____

   _____

   b. _____

   _____

   _____

   c. _____

   _____

   _____

3. Work on the last long sentence together. What do you think Lincoln was saying? Read your guess to the class.

   _____

   _____

   _____

   _____

   _____

Reading

Reading Lincoln's *Gettysburg Address*

In history studies, you sometimes have to study and read speeches and historical documents that can be challenging. Lincoln gave this speech in November of 1863 after the Battle of Gettysburg, where more than 51,000 soldiers from both sides of the Civil War were wounded, missing, or killed. Several versions of the speech exist. It is one of the most frequently quoted speeches in U.S. history. The version printed here matches what is inscribed on the wall of the Lincoln Memorial in Washington, DC. Note that the language used in this speech is not commonly used today.

Transcript of Gettysburg Address (1863)

Fourscore and seven years ago our fathers brought forth on this continent a new nation, conceived in liberty and dedicated to the proposition that all men are created equal.

Now we are engaged in a great civil war, testing whether that nation or any nation so conceived and so dedicated can long endure. We are met on a great battlefield of that war. We have come to dedicate a portion of that field as a final resting place for those who here gave their lives that that nation might live. It is altogether fitting and proper that we should do this.

But in a larger sense, we cannot dedicate, we cannot consecrate, we cannot hallow this ground. The brave men, living and dead who struggled here have consecrated it far above our poor power to add or detract. The world will little note nor long remember what we say here, but it can never forget what they did here. It is for us the living rather to be dedicated here to the unfinished work which they who fought here have thus far so nobly advanced. It is rather for us to be here dedicated to the great task remaining before us—that from these honored dead we take increased devotion to that cause for which they gave the last full measure of devotion—that we here highly resolve that these dead shall not have died in vain, that this nation under God shall have a new birth of freedom, and that government of the people, by the people, for the people shall not perish from the earth.

Listening 1: Listening for Guesses

Listening for Information

The listening passage is a conversation between two students. They are discussing information from their history class about Abraham Lincoln. The students are trying to answer the question that the instructor asked: "What characteristics or events make people list Lincoln as one of the greatest presidents of the United States?" As you listen to the conversation, write answers to the questions.

Listening for Information

1. What phrases do the students use to indicate they're taking a guess?

   _____

   _____

   _____

2. Which student seems more certain? Why do you think so?

   _____

   _____

   _____

3. List words that are linked.

   _____

   _____

   _____

Speaking

Expressing Certainty

Sometimes you are more certain about what you're saying than at other times. When you want the listener to know that you're positive about the information, you can begin your statement with an appropriate phrase. Sometimes you are less certain than other times. There are ways to let your listener know that too.

DEGREES OF CERTAINTY

100% Certain	Less than 100% Certain
I'm certain/sure that	I'm pretty sure that
It is	I am not sure it is
I know that	Could it be
I'm positive that	I'm almost positive that
I'm convinced	I think

Taking Guesses and Expressing Certainty

Think about taking guesses and expressing certainty. Then share your ideas with the class.

1. List three situations when it's okay to take a guess. List three times when you should express certainty.

   _____

   _____

   _____

2. What words do you use to take guesses? To express certainty? Add other phrases to the list and to those on page 102.

   _____

   _____

   _____

3. Are there certain jobs in which people express certainty more than others? Give examples. Is this good, bad, or sometimes good and sometimes bad?

   _____

   _____

   _____

4. What types of things affect a person's decision to take a guess or express certainty? Does the place or time of the interaction matter? Does the formality of the question affect the response? Which phrases are more formal? Which are more informal?

   _____

   _____

   _____

Making Contact

Ask each of the questions to a different English speaker. Take notes on the answers, the phrases (if any) used before the answer in the person's response, and the details of the interaction (person's status, age, and gender, the time of day, and the location). Be prepared to discuss your data with the class.

Question	The Person's Response	Details of the Interaction
Who do you think was the best U.S. president?		
Who gave the Gettysburg Address?		
Who was president during the Civil War?		
How many men were president of the United States before Abraham Lincoln?		
Why do many people think that President Lincoln was a great President?		

Part 2: Richard Nixon

Pre-Listening Activities

Richard Nixon was the 37th president of the United States. During his term (1969–1974), he improved the country's relationships with China and Russia. However, he is remembered mostly because of the Watergate scandal. In 1972, the Democratic Party's office in the Watergate building was broken into, and Nixon, a Republican, was accused of playing a role. The *Washington Post*, a well-known American newspaper, published stories about the Watergate scandal and revealed to the American people that Nixon was involved in this and other similar "tricks" against Democrats. Eventually, Nixon resigned. He was the only president to resign from the presidency. Answer these questions with a partner.

1. What have you heard about the Watergate scandal?

   _____

   _____

2. How do you learn about current events in the news? What newspapers do you read? What websites do you check? Are they reliable?

   _____

   _____

   _____

3. How much freedom should the press (media) have to report anything reporters think is news? Compare freedom of the press in the United States to other countries that you are familiar with.

   _____

   _____

   _____

Strategy: Listening for and Presenting Arguments

In academic discussions, you sometimes have to disagree with someone's opinion. When you do, it's best if you can explain your disagreement and present an argument about why you feel differently. Being able to explain your idea makes it stronger.

There are certain phrases speakers can use to indicate that they are trying to present the other side of an argument or provide details about their ideas. If you listen carefully, you'll be prepared for this new information.

Presenting Arguments

But what about

Don't you agree that

Everyone needs to consider that

I have another [idea/question] we should talk about

The issue is

My point is

The question we need to think about is

Remember that

Well, I think that

What I want to say is

What is important to include is

You're forgetting that

My point is that all citizens have the right to know what the president is doing.

The issue is not about informing us what the person is doing right, it's about knowing that the person has done something wrong.

Don't you agree that sometimes we know too much about other people?

You're forgetting that presidents are elected in the United States, so the people who elect them should know about their activities.

I have another thing we should think about in our discussion of the Constitution.

Pronunciation Note: **Emphatic stress** changes the stress from the main noun to another word. This allows you to emphasize the information you really want your listener to hear.

My point is that **all** citizens have the right to know what the president is doing. [not just some citizens]

My point is that all citizens have the right to know what the **president** is doing. [not all people, just the president]

The issue is not about informing us what the person **is doing right**, it's about us knowing what the person **has done wrong**.

The issue is not about **informing** us what the person is doing right, it's about us **knowing** what the person has done wrong.

Listening for and Presenting Arguments

Work with a partner. Discuss each statement. Take turns giving your opinion and presenting an argument about each. Use emphatic stress as necessary.

1. Abraham Lincoln was the greatest U.S. president.

2. The Eiffel Tower in Paris is the most interesting piece of architecture.

3. McDonald's is the company with the best commercials.

4. *Avatar* was the best movie ever made.

5. Everyone should worry about earthquakes changing the earth's surface.

6. _____ is the best place to go on a vacation.

7. _____ is the best sport to watch.

8. _____ is the best way to study.

9. _____ is the best person to ask for advice.

10. _____ has the friendliest people.

Speaking

Interrupting

During a lecture, you listen more and participate less (if at all). During a discussion, everyone has the right to and should participate. You may have to interrupt to make sure you understood something or to offer your own ideas. Interrupting is okay if it is done politely and at the right time. To be polite, use a friendly intonation and appropriate words. To choose the best time, wait until the speaker has finished an idea. You don't want to interrupt in the middle of a sentence.

There are some polite phrases you can use to interrupt before asking for information or giving your own ideas when possible. Sometimes it is more common to interrupt with one word, especially so you don't miss the opportunity.

Politely Interrupting
Can I say something?
Excuse me.
If I could stop you,
I hate to cut in, but
I have something to add.
I'm sorry, but
I need to interrupt.
Let me jump in.
Pardon me.
Wait.

One-Word Interrupting
ok
no
see
so
well
yeah

Politely Interrupting

Work with a small group. Divide the reading about Richard Nixon on pages 110–11 into four equal parts. Give each person one section of the reading. Write a few notes about your section, and then tell your group members about it. They will politely interrupt you to make sure they understood, to offer their own ideas, or to present an argument. Be prepared to the same when they are sharing their information.

My Notes

_____

_____

_____

_____

_____

_____

_____

_____

_____

_____

_____

_____

_____

_____

_____

_____

_____

_____

_____

Reading

Reading about Richard Nixon's Agenda

Read about Richard Nixon's time in office.

Nixon's Agenda

Reconciliation was the first goal set by President Richard M. Nixon after he won the election. He thought that the nation was painfully divided, with unrest in the cities and the Vietnam War. During his presidency, Nixon improved relations with the Soviet Union (Russia today) and China. Unfortunately, the Watergate scandal brought new divisions to the country and ultimately led to his resignation.

(2) Born in California in 1913, Nixon had a brilliant record at Whittier College and Duke University Law School before beginning to practice law. In 1940, he married Patricia Ryan; they had two daughters, Patricia (Tricia) and Julie. During World War II, Nixon served as a Navy lieutenant commander in the Pacific.

(3) When he left the military, he was elected to Congress from his California district. In 1950, he won a Senate seat. Two years later, General Eisenhower selected Nixon, at age 39, to be his vice president.

(4) As Vice President, Nixon had many responsibilities in the Eisenhower Administration. He was nominated for president in 1960, but he lost to John F. Kennedy. In 1968, he again won his party's nomination and went on to defeat Hubert H. Humphrey and George C. Wallace.

(5) Nixon's accomplishments while in office included the end of the draft (requiring young men to register and serve in the war), new anti-crime laws, and an environmental program.

(6) Some of his best-known achievements came in his quest for world stability. During visits in 1972 to Beijing and Moscow, he reduced tensions with China and the Soviet Union. His meetings with Russian leader Leonid I. Brezhnev produced a treaty to limit strategic nuclear weapons.

(7) In 1972, Nixon was re-elected by defeating Democratic candidate George McGovern.

(8) Within a few months, his administration was embattled over the so-called Watergate scandal, resulting from a break-in at the offices of the Democratic National Committee during the 1972 campaign. The break-in was traced to officials of the Committee to Re-Elect the President. A number of officials resigned; some were later convicted of offenses connected with efforts to cover up the break-in and other crimes. Nixon denied any personal involvement, but the courts forced him to turn in tape recordings that indicated that he had, in fact, known about the activities and later tried to cover them up.

(9) Faced with what seemed almost certain impeachment (dismissal from the presidency), Nixon announced on August 8, 1974, that he would resign the next day to begin "that process of healing which is so desperately needed in America." Gerald Ford was sworn in as the 38th president the next day.

Adapted from *The White House* (whitehouse.gov), "37. Richard M. Nixon, 1969–1974."

Listening 2: Discussing an Issue

Listening in Groups (Video)

Listen to the students talk about Watergate and freedom of the press for their history class. Discuss the questions as a small group.

Focus on Language

1. Do any students take a guess? What wording do they use? <u>Note</u>: Don't worry about writing exact words. Refer to the box on page 98.

   _____

   _____

2. Do any students express certainty? What words do they use? <u>Note</u>: Don't worry about writing exact words. Refer to the box on page 98.

   _____

   _____

3. What are some arguments the students make? What words do they use? <u>Note</u>: Don't worry about writing exact words.

   _____

   _____

4. Do any students interrupt? What words do they use? <u>Note</u>: Don't worry about writing exact words.

   _____

   _____

5. Write any phrases or idioms that you are not familiar with. Discuss what they mean and in what type of interactions they are appropriate.

   _____

   _____

Focus on Tone

1. Do any students use emphatic stress? Write some examples. Are there examples where you think more emphatic stress would be helpful?

   _____

   _____

2. Could you tell by tone which students were guessing and which sounded more certain? Give examples.

   _____

   _____

3. Is each person's tone appropriate? Why or why not?

   _____

   _____

Focus on Nonverbal Communication

1. What nonverbal cues are used to show how each member of the group feels about ideas from other group members?

   _____

   _____

2. Were any of these inappropriate? Why or why not?

   _____

   _____

3. Which student do you think has the most expressive nonverbal communication? Is this good or bad for the interaction?

   _____

   _____

Summary

1. Which student do you think was the most certain? Support your answer.

   _____

   _____

   _____

   _____

2. Which student uses the best combination of words, tone, and nonverbal communication? Is that the person you most agree with? Why or why not?

   _____

   _____

   _____

   _____

3. Which student was the most polite? Support your answer.

   _____

   _____

   _____

   _____

Ranking

The Press Freedom Index is a ranking of countries that have the most freedom of the press. An organization called Reporters without Borders gives a survey and ranking to all the countries.

Work with a group, and guess which countries you think have the most freedom of the press.

Our Guesses:

_____

_____

_____

_____

Look at this list of 22 countries. Of these, which five countries made the list of countries having the most freedom of the press and which five countries are thought to have the least freedom of the press?

Australia	Finland	Lithuania	Sweden
Austria	Germany	Luxembourg	Switzerland
Belgium	Iceland	Malta	United Kingdom
Canada	Ireland	Netherlands	United States
Denmark	Japan	New Zeland	of America
Estonia	Latvia	Norway	

Our Ranking

TOP 5	BOTTOM 5
_____	_____
_____	_____
_____	_____
_____	_____
_____	_____

Information gathered from *Reporters without Borders for Press Freedom*, "Press Freedom Index 2009," http://en.rsf.org/spip.php?page=classement&id_rubrique=1001.

Part 3: John F. Kennedy

Pre-Listening Activities

John F. Kennedy was the 35th president of the United States. His presidency ended when he was assassinated on November 22, 1963, in Dallas, Texas. Although he was only president for three years, from 1961 to 1963, he made several significant decisions, and his term was marked by events that are still important in the United States today. Answer these questions with a partner.

1. What do you know about John F. Kennedy?

   _____

   _____

   _____

2. How important do you think space exploration has been to our world?

   _____

   _____

   _____

3. Name one historical event that you can explain well. What was the event? Where and when did it take place? What caused this event? Why is this historical event important to us today?

   _____

   _____

   _____

Strategy: Listening for and Using Cause-and-Effect Signal Words and Phrases

Speakers often describe important events by explaining who was involved and where and when the event happened. They also describe **how** the event happened and its **cause** (why) and **effect** (the **result** or its significance). They use signal words and phrases to describe those conditions. Noticing these words and phrases will help you take notes during lectures and organize them into event charts to study from later.

Cause-and-Effect Signal Words and Phrases

as	owing to
as a result	resulting from
because	since
because of	so
consequently	so that
due to	therefore
in order to	thus

As a boy, he attended a boarding school in Connecticut, but he got sick. Therefore, he had to leave school to recover from his surgery.

Kennedy's thesis on England was published in part because his father wanted him to publish it as a book.

Kennedy volunteered to be in the U.S. Navy, but, as a result of his back problems, he was not accepted at first.

Kennedy's older brother Joe was going to be the politician in the family. Joe was killed in World War II. Thus, John Kennedy ran for Congress in 1948 when James Michael Curley left his seat to become the Mayor of Boston.

What others can you think of to add to the list?

Using Cause-and-Effect Signal Words and Phrases

Read the sentences in the left column. For each, choose the detail that is a cause or effect of it from the right column.

1. _____ Lincoln didn't have an easy life. He had to work all day on the farm and then at other jobs.

2. _____ Lincoln ran for political office as someone who was against slavery.

3. _____ The man that shot Lincoln thought he could help the South in the Civil War.

4. _____ In 1864, people wanted Lincoln to keep leading the country.

5. _____ Lincoln had only one son that lived to be an adult.

a. He was re-elected before the war ended.

b. He didn't get to go to school like other children.

c. He learned to get through hard times.

d. As president, he signed the Emancipation Proclamation that freed the slaves.

e. He shot Lincoln at Ford's Theatre on April 14, 1865.

What words would you use to connect each one? Write a sentence (or two) connecting the ideas using a cause-and-result signal word or phrase from the box on page 117. Note that some rewording may be necessary depending on which continuation signal word or phrase you choose.

1. _____

_____

2. _____

_____

3. _____

_____

4. _____

_____

5. _____

_____

Note-Taking

Strategy: Using an Event Chart

An event chart is a graphic organizer that you can use while you take notes or later to help you organize them. Event charts are ideal for making sure you have all the relevant information about the topics being discussed. Empty places on your chart let you know what you can ask about later or look up in your textbook or online.

Event charts can be designed different ways. Some have the event in a circle in the middle and other circles that extend from it so you can fill in details about who, when, where, why (cause), how, and its significance (result). Others list the event and then leave room for the details (the causes or reasons for it) and then list the significance or results. A third type looks like a chart.

WHAT was the EVENT? _____	
WHO was involved?	
WHERE did it happen?	
WHEN did it happen?	
WHY did it happen (its cause)?	
HOW did it happen?	
SIGNIFICANCE (its result)?	

Vocabulary Power

There are a number of terms and phrases in this lecture that you may encounter in other academic settings. Add at least five vocabulary items to your vocabulary notebook or log.

Match the words in bold from the lecture on the left with a definition on the right.

1. _____ The first two **significant** events—starting the Peace Corps and being against war —were alluded to immediately during his inaugural address as he was sworn in.

2. _____ So, Kennedy gave many famous speeches, but one memorable quotation that many Americans to this day can **quote** directly came from his very first speech as President of the United States.

3. _____ Peace Corps volunteers have college degrees and help **fulfill** the goals of the Peace Corps.

4. _____ To **prevent** further contamination by nuclear weapons, he suggested the Partial Test Ban Treaty.

5. _____ This **treaty** stopped testing of atomic bombs on the ground, in the atmosphere or air, or under the water.

6. _____ . . . Kennedy approached the Soviet Union about a **joint** venture.

7. _____ . . . the U.S. had an **obligation** to be first.

8. _____ Six years later, we were able to realize this goal when men **set** foot on the moon. . . .

a. important

b. agreement

c. stop from happening

d. meet; complete

e. responsibility

f. put

g. state

h. combined

Listening 3: John F. Kennedy's Legacy

Listening to a Lecture

The listening passage is a lecture from a U.S. history class focusing on the 20th century. The instructor is talking about significant events and decisions that Kennedy made during his term as president. As you listen, take notes. Then try to organize your notes into an event chart. Use a separate sheet of paper for each event.

Checking Your Understanding: Main Ideas

Review your notes and event charts. Listen again to the lecture if necessary, and then put a check mark (✓) next to the statements that best reflect the main ideas.

1. _____ Kennedy gave many famous speeches.

2. _____ Kennedy felt Americans needed to be more active outside the United States, so he started the Peace Corps.

3. _____ Kennedy wanted to prevent wars.

4. _____ Kennedy was against tyranny, poverty, and disease.

5. _____ Kennedy wanted the United States to be a leader in space exploration.

Checking Your Understanding: Details

Use your notes and event charts, and put a check mark (✓) next to the best answer. Some questions have more than one answer.

1. Who played a role in starting the Peace Corps?

   a. _____ Kennedy

   b. _____ all Americans

   c. _____ Congress

2. What probably made Kennedy so determined to prevent war?

   a. _____ common enemies of man

   b. _____ radioactive contamination

   c. _____ the dangers of nuclear weapons

   d. _____ his own military experience

3. What was significant about the Partial Treaty Ban?

   a. _____ It stopped testing of atomic bombs only on the ground.

   b. _____ It was signed by the Soviet Union.

   c. _____ It was the cause of his own boat sinking.

   d. _____ It never became a law.

4. What places were involved in Kennedy talking about the space program?

   a. _____ Houston

   b. _____ Soviet Union

   c. _____ the Ukraine

   d. _____ China

5. When was the goal of the U.S. space mission finally accomplished?

   a. _____ when Kruschchev signed the agreement in 1963

   b. _____ when Kennedy talked at Rice University in 1962

   c. _____ six years after Kennedy's death in 1969

   d. _____ when Kennedy was assassinated in 1963

In-Depth Discussion

Work with a small group. Imagine your group is taking historical notes on a former president or leader that is starting his or her own museum. Talk about these details and then present the information about your president to the rest of the class.

1. Who is your leader? Give some details about his or her personal life.

   _____

   _____

2. Where was your leader from, and what country did he or she lead?

   _____

   _____

3. What leadership qualities did he or she have?

   _____

   _____

4. What significant events did your leader manage?

   _____

   _____

5. What important decisions did your leader have to make?

   _____

   _____

6. What were the results of your leader's events or decisions?

   _____

   _____

7. What will your leader be most remembered for?

   _____

   _____

8. Where will the museum be located, and what will it look like?

   _____

   _____

Rapid Vocabulary Review

From the three answers on the right, circle the one that best explains, is an example of, or combines with the vocabulary item on the left as it is used in this unit.

Vocabulary	Answers		
Synonyms			
1. perish	die	listen	weaken
2. brave	not afraid	not happy	not sleepy
3. compromise	agree	understand	meet halfway
4. a transcript	food	people	words
5. reveal	not believe	not damage	not hide
6. fitting	appropriate	impact	skeleton
7. disseminate	distribute	retain	urge
8. positive	certain	necessary	wrong
9. deny	say no	say maybe	say yes
10. wounded	approximate, almost	hurt, injured	sure, certain
11. reliable	countable	dependable	predictable
12. a portion	a contract	a piece of furniture	a part
Combinations and Associations			
13. ___ a guess	do	let	take
14. disagree ___ someone	at	for	with
15. let me ___ in	choose	jump	precede
16. ___ sure	beautiful	cute	pretty
17. ___ on more duties	make	put	take
18. a teaching ___	career	family	weather
19. ___ a person's decision	affect	make	run
20. run ___ a political office	for	in	to

⇨✕⇦ **Synthesizing: Projects and Presentations**

Short In-Class Speaking Assignments	Longer Outside Assignments
Freedom of the Press	**Current Events**
Bring in a news article from a local newspaper (or printed from an online news source). With a small group, decide if your article is from a good, reliable source. Talk about the topic covered, and decide if the topic is one that everyone should know about or if the press is giving information that is not based on fact. Finally, decide how much freedom the press should have.	Divide the class into two teams, and make a list of current events at your school, in your city, or in the world. One team will make a list of positive aspects of the events. The other team will make a list of the negative aspects. Take turns presenting your arguments to the other team. Make sure to use the best phrases when you are guessing and when you are expressing certainty. Be prepared for your classmates to interrupt if they have information to add.
World Events	**Presidential Presentation**
Work with a group. Make a list of the ten events that you think are most important in world history. Rank them in order with the most important being number one. Give at least one reason why each one is on the top ten list.	Choose one U.S. president, and research details about his life. Choose a significant event that took place during the presidency. Be sure to discuss the causes and results of the decisions. Make a presentation that includes the details. Express certainty when you are stating facts, and let your listeners know if you are making guesses.

Vocabulary Log

To increase your vocabulary knowledge, write a definition or translation for each vocabulary item. Then write an original phrase, sentence, or note that will help you remember the vocabulary item.

Vocabulary Item	Definition or Translation	Your Original Phrase, Sentence, or Note
1. missing	not present, not here	My keys are missing.
2. a response		
3. brilliant		
4. slavery		
5. ambition		
6. resign		
7. a version		
8. improve		
9. in vain		
10. challenging		
11. reject		
12. prompt (v.)		
13. thus		

Vocabulary Item	Definition or Translation	Your Original Phrase, Sentence, or Note
14. vision		
15. a duty		
16. a document		
17. heal		
18. campaign		
19. a treaty		
20. a scandal		
21. struggle		
22. partial		
23. assassinate		
24. a journalist		
25. the draft		

5 Chemistry: The Elements

Chemistry is a science that studies whatobjects are made of and how they change when chemicals are involved. The study of chemistry has existed for a long time. Some records date it back to the ancient Egyptians of 4,000 years ago. This unit will talk about chemical elements and how they are studied today.

Part 1: Green Chemistry

Pre-Listening Activities

An element is a chemical substance that has one kind of atom. Some common elements include gold, oxygen, iron, or sodium. To date, more than 115 elements have been discovered. A more recent field is green chemistry. Green chemists want to make the environment better by developing solutions for existing problems. Answer these questions with a partner.

1. What do you think the earth's biggest environmental problems are?

   _____

   _____

   _____

2. How do you think chemicals positively and/or negatively affect the environment?

   _____

   _____

   _____

3. What solutions can you think of for one of problems you discussed in Question 1?

   _____

   _____

   _____

Strategy: Listening for and Giving Opinions

In Unit 3, you learned some ways that speakers let you know that an interesting fact is being given. In Unit 4, you learned that speakers can let you know when they are taking guesses or expressing certainty. Sometimes in conversations or academic discussions, speakers will want to give their opinion. Listen for certain words or phrases so you'll recognize when someone is giving an opinion instead of a fact.

Giving Opinions

As I see it

If you ask me

In my opinion

I think/believe/feel

Personally, I think

To my mind

To me

Sometimes speakers will ask you for your opinion. Listen for these questions.

Asking for Opinions

What do you think about

Do you have any feelings about

What are your thoughts about

How do you feel about

What's your opinion about

> **Personally, I think** the earth's biggest environmental problem is pollution. What do you think?
>
> **To my mind,** more needs to be done to find other types of fuel. What are your thoughts about this?
>
> **If you ask me,** not enough recycling bins are on campus. What is your opinion?

Pronunciation Note: In English words with more than one syllable, one receives more stress than the others. This is called the **primary** stress. The primary stress is usually in the content words. Stressing these syllables will help you achieve the rhythm of English.

<u>Pers</u>onally, I feel the earth's <u>big</u>gest en<u>vi</u>ronmental <u>pro</u>blem is pol<u>lu</u>tion.

Listening for and Giving Opinions

Work with a partner. Take turns asking for and giving opinions on the topics. Practice using primary stress in words that have more than one syllable.

1. your favorite building on campus

2. the best television show

3. the hardest thing about learning English

4. the easiest class you've taken

5. the best thing about your school

6. using cell phones while driving

7. the amount of homework you have

8. smoking in restaurants

9. school uniforms

10. professional athletes

Speaking

Asking for an Explanation

When you need more information, you have to ask for it. Do not be afraid to ask for an explanation from someone. This is good to do during any conversation when you need more information, but it is especially important during academic discussions so you can make sure you get more information or understand important information. There are a few ways to ask indirectly (by using a statement), but more ways to be direct (by asking a question).

ASKING FOR AN EXPLANATION, DIRECT AND INDIRECT

Statements	Questions
I'm not sure I know/understand.	What do you mean?
I need more information.	Do you mean?
I don't see why	Can you explain?
I can't see a reason for	Why [is that a good idea] [does that happen]?
There must be a reason for	Why is that true?
I wonder about	What does that mean
I'm curious about	For what reason?
I don't get it.	This happened because? (rising intonation on *because*)
Hmm	Could you be more specific about
Excuse me, I'm not following this.	Can you talk a little about
I don't understand why this is important.	Could you talk more about
I have a question.	Could you give an example of that?
I'd like to know more.	I'm sorry, could I ask one last thing about that one?
I'm not sure what that meant.	How?/How come?

Reading

Read some information about why hydrogen is a good chemical element that is being used in ways to help the environment in California. This reading may seem challenging, but it will be a good way to practice asking for explanations during an academic discussion or after a lecture. As you read this information, ask yourself whether this information applies to your local setting.

Why Hydrogen?

Hydrogen has many important advantages over other fuels. Hydrogen can be made from renewable sources. It is clean to use. It is the fuel of choice for energy-efficient fuel cells. Hydrogen is first on the periodic table of the elements. It is the least complex and most abundant element in the universe. Hydrogen will play a critical role in a new, decentralized energy infrastructure that can provide power to vehicles, homes, and industries. Hydrogen has the ability to address several high-priority areas for California:

- Energy security and diversity: Hydrogen can be produced from a variety of domestic sources, including renewable sources. This enables diversification of our energy supply, especially in the transportation sector, which is currently almost 100% dependent on petroleum fuels.

- Synergy among energy use sectors: Hydrogen "energy stations" can provide heating, cooling, and power for homes and businesses. At the same time, it can co-produce hydrogen for use in vehicles. As an energy carrier, hydrogen can store, move, and deliver energy in a usable form to consumers. This useful attribute can help improve and stabilize the ways our electricity system meets growing consumer demand.

- Environmental protection: Hydrogen fuel can be used in vehicles powered by either internal combustion engines or fuel cells. This results in near-zero or zero tailpipe emissions. When hydrogen is produced from renewable resources and used to power fuel cell vehicles, the entire chain of processes (fuel production through end use in a vehicle) results in extremely low environmental impacts.

- Economic development: California has long been at the forefront of emerging high-technology industries. State officials have recognized that early support for these industries can translate into job-creation benefits as technologies flourish in the marketplace.

Adapted from *State of California*, "California Hydrogen Highway FAQS, 2010."

Asking for Explanations

Write four specific questions asking for explanations about information in the reading.

a. _____

_____

b. _____

_____

c. _____

_____

d. _____

_____

Answer these questions with a partner.

1. What kind of information did you decide you wanted an explanation about? What phrases did you use to ask?

_____

_____

2. Are some phrases more formal than others? Which do you consider more formal? Which are less formal?

_____

_____

3. What statements or questions do you use? Can you add any others?

_____

_____

4. What things affect the phrasing you choose? Does the place or time of the interaction matter? Does it matter who you are asking?

_____

_____

Listening 1: Listening to an Academic Presentation

Listening for Information

The listening passage is the beginning of an academic talk. A chemist is visiting the school and giving a talk about hydrogen. A couple of times, audience members ask questions. As you listen to the presentation and questions, answer the questions.

Listening for Information

1. Which items do audience members ask for explanations about? (Circle all that apply.)

   a. electrolysis

   b. lower emissions

   c. why it's better to use hydrogen

   d. what bad emissions are

   e. flammability

   f. price

   g. other industries using hydrogen

2. Which of the topics were the speaker's opinion? (Circle all that apply.)

   a. what hydrogen is made from

   b. one of the best uses for hydrogen

   c. the most important reason for using hydrogen

   d. why it's better to use hydrogen

   e. how hydrogen ignites

   f. the price of gasoline

   g. car makers eventually selling hydrogen-powered cars

3. Listen again. What words or phrases are used to ask for explanations, ask for opinions, and give opinions? <u>Note</u>: Don't worry about writing exact words.

Ask for Explanations	Ask for Opinions	Give Opinions

Making Contact

Survey three people. Ask their opinions about cars. Take notes on their answers and the phrases (if any) they use. Complete the chart, and be prepared to combine your results with four classmates and present those to the class.

Person's Name	Person 1 _____	Person 2 _____	Person 3 _____
What do you think is the best car to buy?			
What is your opinion about cars that don't use gasoline?			
What do you think about the price of cars?			

Part 2: The Periodic Table of Elements

Pre-Listening Activities

Part 1 talked about one element, hydrogen, and how it can help the environment. Part 2 is about the periodic table. The periodic table is a reference that lists all current chemical elements by their atomic number (for example, how many protons are in an atom). Chemists use the periodic table to learn information about individual elements and how they behave. The periodic table is updated when new elements are discovered. Answer these questions with a partner.

1. List any chemical elements you know.

   _____

   _____

   _____

2. The symbol for hydrogen is H. Do you know any symbols for the other elements? List any you know.

   _____

   _____

   _____

3. Why do you think it is important to be able to see all the elements on one chart?

   _____

   _____

   _____

Legend:

14
Si
28.086
Silicon

atomic number → (top left)
symbol → Si
name → Silicon

Periodic Table of the Elements

1 **H** Hydrogen																		2 **He** Helium
3 **Li** Lithium	4 **Be** Beryllium											5 **B** Boron	6 **C** Carbon	7 **N** Nitrogen	8 **O** Oxygen	9 **F** Fluorine	10 **Ne** Neon
11 **Na** Sodium	12 **Mg** Magnesium											13 **Al** Aluminium	14 **Si** Silicon	15 **P** Phosphorus	16 **S** Sulfur	17 **Cl** Chlorine	18 **Ar** Argon
19 **K** Potassium	20 **Ca** Calcium	21 **Sc** Scandium	22 **Ti** Titanium	23 **V** Vanadium	24 **Cr** Chromium	25 **Mn** Manganese	26 **Fe** Iron	27 **Co** Cobalt	28 **Ni** Nickel	29 **Cu** Copper	30 **Zn** Zinc	31 **Ga** Gallium	32 **Ge** Germanium	33 **As** Arsenic	34 **Se** Selenium	35 **Br** Bromine	36 **Kr** Krypton
37 **Rb** Rubidium	38 **Si** Strontium	39 **Y** Yttrium	40 **Zr** Zirconium	41 **Nb** Niobium	42 **Mo** Molybdenum	43 **Tc** Technetium	44 **Ru** Ruthenium	45 **Rh** Rhodium	46 **Pd** Palladium	47 **Ag** Silver	48 **Cd** Cadmium	49 **In** Indium	50 **Sn** Tin	51 **Sb** Antimony	52 **Te** Tellurium	53 **I** Iodine	54 **Xe** Xenon
55 **Cs** Caesium	56 **Ba** Barium	57 **La** Lanthanide	72 **Hf** Hafnium	73 **Ta** Tantalum	74 **W** Tungsten	75 **Re** Rhenium	76 **Os** Osmium	77 **Ir** Iridium	78 **Pt** Platinum	79 **Au** Gold	80 **Hg** Mercury	81 **Tl** Thallium	82 **Pb** Lead	83 **Bi** Bismuth	84 **Po** Polonium	85 **At** Astatine	86 **Rn** Radon
87 **Fr** Francium	88 **Ra** Radium	89 **Ac** Actinide	104 **Rf** Rutherfordium	105 **Db** Dubnium	106 **Sg** Seaborgium	107 **Bh** Bohrium	108 **Hs** Hassium	109 **Mt** Meitnerium	110 **Ds** Darmstadtium	111 **Rg** Roentgenium	112 **Cn** Copernicium	113 **Uut** Niobium	114 **Uuq** Ununquadium	115 **Uup** Niobium	116 **Uuh** Niobium	117 **Uus** Niobium	118 **Uuo** Niobium

Lanthanoids

58 **Ce** Cerium	59 **Pr** Praseodymium	60 **Nd** Neodymium	61 **Pm** Promethium	62 **Sm** Samarium	63 **Eu** Europium	64 **Gd** Gadolinium	65 **Tb** Terbium	66 **Dy** Dysprosium	67 **Ho** Holmium	68 **Er** Erbium	69 **Tm** Thulium	70 **Yb** Yttersium	71 **Lu** Lutetium

Actinoids

90 **Th** Thorium	91 **Pa** Protactinium	92 **U** Uranium	93 **Np** Neptunium	94 **Pu** Plutonium	95 **Am** Americium	96 **Cm** Curium	97 **Bk** Berkelium	98 **Cf** Californium	99 **Es** Einsteinium	100 **Fm** Fermium	101 **Md** Mendelevium	102 **No** Nobelium	103 **Lr** Lawrencium

Strategy: Listening for and Using Spatial Signal Words and Phrases

Some academic discussions and lectures describe a place or an illustration. To give you a mental picture or help you find something in a physical picture, speakers will use spatial words or phrases to guide the listeners. There are many words and phrases that describe where something is.

Spatial Signal Words and Phrases

above	close (to)
across (from)	far (from)
adjacent (to)	in
after	inside
at	near
behind	next to
below	on
beside	outside
between	to the left (of)
by	to the right (of)
centered	under

More than one spatial word or phrase can be used in a sentence.

Neon is **in** the row **below** helium.

Cobalt is **near** nickel and **centered** in the fourth row.

Many spatial words and phrases are used as part of prepositional phrases.

Hydrogen is **at the top** of the periodic table.

Neon is **in the row** below helium.

Pronunciation Note: In prepositional phrases, the object of the preposition receives the main stress. As a speaker, you need to decide how important the spatial word is. If you use it as part of a prepositional phrase (as in *in the row*), you will not stress it. Therefore, you need to listen carefully for spatial signals.

Nickel is in the fourth **ROW** **not** Neon is **IN** the fourth row.

Using Spatial Signal Words and Phrases

Write descriptions of the locations using spatial words and phrases. Be as detailed as you can. Then compare your answers with a partner.

1. your classroom

   _____

   _____

   _____

   _____

   _____

2. locations of these buildings on campus (or any five places in your building): the library, the student union, the bookstore, the registrar's office, your teacher's office

   _____

   _____

   _____

   _____

   _____

3. directions from school to the closest restaurant

   _____

   _____

   _____

   _____

   _____

Speaking

Confirming Correct or Incorrect

When people are explaining or describing things, people may ask if they have things right or wrong. Some common ways to ask are, *Is this correct?* or *Did I do this the right way?* Speakers will then confirm if the listener is right or wrong. Tone of voice is extremely important. Even if the other person is wrong, you don't want to make that person feel bad. There are many phrases you can use.

CONFIRMING CORRECT OR INCORRECT

Correct	Incorrect
Yes. / Yep.	No.
That's right.	No, sorry, that's not right.
Right.	Nope. That's not it.
Exactly.	Close, but not exactly. Sort of, but not exactly. Kind of, but not exactly.
Yes, correct.	Sorry.
Perfect.	Not exactly, no.
Okay.	Nope.
You've got it.	Unfortunately, that's not right.

Role-Playing

Work with a partner to role play possible conversations for these situations. Use the phrases in the box on page 139 or others that you can think of to write dialogues. Then exchange roles. Read your dialogues to the class.

SITUATIONS

providing directions from the classroom to your home

giving advice on what to do when you have a cold

describing a process in your field of study

Person A begins by giving directions or advice, describing the process, or listing ideas.

Person B repeats or paraphrases Person A's comments. Person B can also ask for an explanation or more information by using phrases from the box on page 132.

Person A confirms whether Person B is correct or incorrect.

Person A:

_____

_____

_____

_____

Person B:

_____

_____

_____

_____

Person A:

_____

If Person B is incorrect or not exact, Person A can explain again, so Person B has another chance. If Person B is exactly correct, then switch roles.

Listening 2: Describing and Confirming

Listening in Pairs (Video)

Listen to the pair of students studying for a chemistry test. They are referring to the periodic table of elements. Discuss the questions with a small group.

Focus on Language

1. What words or phrases do the students use when they give an opinion? <u>Note</u>: Refer to the box on page 130. Don't worry about writing exact words.

    _____

    _____

2. Do any students ask for an explanation? What words do they use? Refer to the box on page 130. <u>Note</u>: Don't worry about writing exact words.

    _____

    _____

3. Where are the elements they talk about on the periodic table?

    _____

    _____

4. What confirmations for correct or incorrect are used? <u>Note</u>: Don't worry about writing exact words.

    _____

    _____

5. Write any phrases or idioms that you are not familiar with. Discuss what they mean and in what type of interactions they are appropriate.

    _____

    _____

Focus on Tone

1. Who do you think uses the best tone of voice? Why do you like this person's tone best?

   _____

   _____

2. Is each person's tone appropriate? Why or why not?

   _____

   _____

3. List the prepositional phrases you hear. Which words are stressed most in the phrases?

   _____

   _____

Focus on Nonverbal Communication

1. What nonverbal cues are used to show how each person feels during the discussion?

    _____

    _____

2. Was any nonverbal communication inappropriate? Why or why not?

    _____

    _____

3. Which student do you think has the most expressive facial expressions? Is this good or bad for the interaction?

    _____

    _____

Summary

1. Which student does a better job of using spatial words and phrases? Give a reason for your opinion.

   _____

   _____

   _____

   _____

2. Which student uses the best combination of words, tone, and nonverbal communication? Support your answer.

   _____

   _____

   _____

   _____

3. Who would you most want to work with? Why? Who would you rather not work with? Why?

   _____

   _____

   _____

   _____

Information Gap

The chemical elements are organized into the Periodic Table. The elements are arranged from left to right and top to bottom. They are in order from the lowest to the highest atomic number.

Work with a partner to complete the missing information about the elements in the chart in the first three columns. Complete the last column of the chart together by finding the element in the current period table on page 138 and describing its location using spatial signals. Confirm correct and incorrect as needed. When you're finished, a sample row would look like this:

Atomic Number	Symbol	Name	Location
21	Sc	Scandium	fourth row, third from the left

Atomic Number	Symbol	Name	Location
1	H	Hydrogen	
6	C		
	Na	Sodium	
14		Silicon	
	Ti	Titanium	
29	Cu		
	Ag		
50		Tin	
79		Gold	
80	Hg		
	Rn	Radon	
88	Ra	Radium	

Atomic Number	Symbol	Name	Location
1	H	Hydrogen	
6		Carbon	
11	Na		
	Si	Silicon	
22	Ti		
29		Copper	
47		Silver	
50		Tin	
79	Au		
80	Hg	Mercury	
86			
	Ra	Radium	

Part 3: Ocean Acidification

Pre-Listening Activities

Depending on who you ask, there are four or five oceans on Earth. These oceans cover approximately 70 percent of the surface. The oceans are important because they affect weather, temperature, and climate change. Although oceans are often studied as part of Earth Science, there are some things about oceans that are studied in chemistry. Answer these questions with a partner.

1. How many oceans can you name? List them. Do you know where they are?

   _____

   _____

   _____

2. How many oceans have you seen? If you have seen more than one, did they look the same? Different? If so, in what ways?

   _____

   _____

   _____

3. Do you know what elements are combined to make water? What about carbon dioxide?

   _____

   _____

   _____

Strategy: Listening for and Using Changing-the-Topic Signal Words and Phrases

Some instructors will give you a lot of information in one lecture. Although the topics may be related, the instructors will let you know when they are changing it completely or taking the topic in a new direction. Listening for specific signal words or phrases will let you know when you should be prepared for a new topic or to start a new set of notes.

Change-of-Topic Signal Words or Phrases

Moving on,

Now,

Speaking of

Keep that in mind (as we now talk about)

That reminds me,

By the way,

The next [element]

> Ocean waters cover approximately 70 percent of the Earth's surface. One is connected body of salt water called the World Ocean. Some people say the World Ocean is divided into five smaller oceans. **By the way**, the Pacific Ocean is considered the largest of these. The Pacific Ocean. . . .
>
> The Pacific Ocean separates Asia and Australia from North and South America. It is the largest ocean. It covers approximately one-third of the surface of the planet and is much larger than all the land on Earth. It's over 63 million square miles. Try to visualize how large that is. **Moving on** to the Atlantic Ocean. . . .

What others can you think of to add to the list?

Listening for and Using Change-of-Topic Signal Words and Phrases

Work with a partner. Look at the chains listed. The first person will state an opinion, give a fact, take a guess, or express certainty about the first item in the chain. The second person will try to make a smooth transition to the next topic in the chain using an appropriate signal word or phrase. Reverse roles. One has been done for you.

English class	→	Last weekend	→	Job

A: English class was really interesting today, but we have a lot of homework to do.

B: Speaking of homework, I spent all of last weekend doing homework. It was terrible, especially since I had to work too.

A: That reminds me. I won't be able to study a lot this weekend because I'm starting my new job.

1.

Atlantic Ocean	→	Research paper	→	Roommate

A: _____

B: _____

A: _____

2.

Newspaper	→	Football game	→	Earth Science

A: _____

B: _____

A: _____

3.

Architecture	→	A study group	→	New shirt

A: _____

B: _____

A: _____

Note-Taking

Strategy: Using a Spider Chart for Related Topics

Many lectures are about one general topic, but they cover a lot of subtopics. Speakers will often use the signal words and phrases to let you know when a related topic is starting. A spider chart works well when the topic changes several times. You can use this as you are taking notes or to organize your notes after the lecture when you are studying.

Spider charts can be drawn many ways. A common spider chart looks like this.

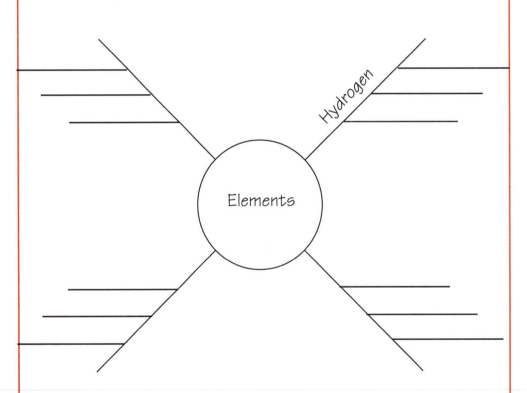

The middle circle is for the lecture title or main topic. The long lines are for each subtopic indicated by a change of topic signal word or phrase. Details can be added to the other lines extending from each subtopic. You can also add "legs" to your spider chart if there are more subtopics.

Creating a Spider Chart

Work with a group. Make a spider chart for one of the conversations you had for the activity on page 151. Add details that a person could talk about for each of the subtopics, and add one more subtopic to your spider chart. Be prepared to show your spider chart to the class.

Vocabulary Power

There are a number of terms and phrases in this lecture that you may encounter in other academic settings. Add at least five vocabulary items to your vocabulary notebook or log.

Match the words in bold from the lecture on the left with a definition on the right.

1. _____ Keep that in mind as I spend a little time talking about the **rate** of acidification.

2. _____ . . . it's expected to **keep** dropping to perhaps 7.949 by the year 2050.

3. _____ The oceans will **get** more and more acidic.

4. _____ It seems like a small drop, but many scientists are **concerned**.

5. _____ When it **dissolves** in seawater, the amount of hydrogen ion concentration rises.

6. _____ Some animals that are **affected** are mussels and snails.

7. _____ If one animal species that is the food **source** for another disappears, won't another be forced to change, or worse, disappear?

8. _____ They will also be more **delicate,** and they could erode faster.

a. changed

b. become

c. origin

d. easy to break

e. break into pieces

f. speed (over time)

g. worried

h. continue

Listening 3: Ocean Acidification

Listening to a Lecture

The listening passage is a lecture from an introductory chemistry class about ocean acidification, what it means, and how it is affecting the oceans. Throughout the lecture, the instructor moves on by discussing some related topics. Listen two times. The first time, take notes as you would normally. Then create a spider chart on a separate piece of paper based on the information. Complete the chart with the information you have. Then listen again, adding more details to your chart.

Checking Your Understanding: Main Ideas

Review your notes. Listen again to the lecture if necessary, and then put a check mark (✓) next to the statements that best reflect the main ideas.

1. _____ The chemistry of the oceans is changing.

2. _____ The chemical changes could negatively affect marine and human life.

3. _____ Less carbonate is available to marine life.

4. _____ Humans are causing and will suffer from increased carbon dioxide.

5. _____ The acidity of the oceans could eventually be the same as lemon juice.

Checking Your Understanding: Details

Use your notes, and put a check mark (✓) next to the best answer. Some questions have more than one answer.

1. What is the main topic of the lecture?

   a. _____ ocean acidification

   b. _____ the rate of acidification

   c. _____ the impacts of acidification

   d. _____ the change to marine life of acidification

   e. _____ basic versus acid

2. What subtopics are covered?

   a. _____ ocean acidification

   b. _____ rate of acidification

   c. _____ industrialized world

   d. _____ how acidification happens

   e. _____ how marine life makes skeletons from $CaCO_3$

   f. _____ the impact on human life

   g. _____ items on the basic pH scale

3. What effects might ocean acidification have on marine life?

   a. _____ coral reefs will grow more slowly

   b. _____ animals won't be able to make their skeletons

   c. _____ food sources for other animals might disappear

4. How might humans be affected by changes to marine life?

   a. _____ coral reefs will stop growing and tourism will fall

   b. _____ snails won't be considered a delicacy anymore

   c. _____ the food industry will suffer

5. What items are mentioned as acidic?

   a. _____ lemon juice

   b. _____ water

   c. _____ sea water

   d. _____ tomato juice

   e. _____ ammonia

   f. _____ baking soda

   g. _____ battery acid

In-Depth Discussion

Work with a small group. Imagine you are part of a team of chemists that has been asked to answer some questions about the future. Think of an answer to each question about chemistry. When you are finished, take turns serving on a panel to discuss your opinions.

1. What will happen if ocean acidification continues and marine life can no longer live?

   _____

   _____

2. When will there be more cars that run on hydrogen or electricity than on gasoline?

   _____

   _____

3. Which chemical element do you think will be the most important in the future? Why?

   _____

   _____

4. What predictions can you make about the future of the environment?

   _____

   _____

5. What three foods do you think are the most acidic?

   _____

   _____

6. What do you think of the field chemistry should study next?

   _____

   _____

7. Do you think all students should be required to take a chemistry class? Why or why not?

   _____

   _____

Rapid Vocabulary Review

From the three answers on the right, circle the one that best explains, is an example of, or combines with the vocabulary item on the left as it is used in this unit.

Vocabulary	Answers		
Synonyms			
1. store (v.)	decide	keep	mention
2. a skeleton	bones	chains	surfaces
3. How come?	How?	When?	Why?
4. ignite	burn	guess	treat
5. reverse	backward	forward	signal
6. the source	the second part	the origin	the question
7. a vehicle	a number	an element	a car
8. ancient	very nervous	very old	very polite
9. behave	act	expose	shift
10. flourish	behave badly	not move	grow well
11. subtle	not true	small	wonderful
12. a snail	an animal	a chemical	a plant
Combinations and Associations			
13. keep that ___ mind	of	in	on
14. that reminds ___	chemistry	me	the event
15. ___ to	adjacent	beside	under
16. approximately ___	the morning	the 1700s	1,700
17. a ___ transition	friend's	nitrogen	smooth
18. a recycling ___	adult	bin	careful
19. on a different ___	mind	note	opinion
20. X is close ___ Y	from	near	to

⇨✕⊐ Synthesizing: Projects and Presentations

Short In-Class Speaking Assignments	Longer Outside Assignments
Where in the World?	**Spider Chart Posters**
Think of a location. It should be a place that your classmates are familiar with. It could be somewhere on campus, a place in the city, or a well-known city anywhere in the world. Your classmates will have a chance to ask questions as they try to guess the place you are thinking of. For example, they might say, "Is it in the U.S.?" You will have to confirm if each guess is correct or incorrect. Give your classmates 20 questions to guess correctly.	Imagine you have the chance to present a poster session at a chemistry conference. Prepare a spider chart poster. Choose an element from the periodic table. Then decide on four subtopics about the element and three details for each. Create your spider chart poster to present to the rest of the class. Be prepared to answer a few questions when your classmates ask for an explanation and give explanations and confirm correctness or incorrectness when your classmates ask questions.
Change the Topic	**Helping the Environment**
Sit in a circle with three or four classmates. The first person should state an opinion about a current event at school or in the world based on the school newspaper or an event in the news. The next person can respond by asking for an explanation or more information OR by changing the topic (and stating an opinion about the new topic). Continue around the circle several times. When you finish, discuss how many times the subject changed, and discuss your reasons for the changes in topic when they happened.	Do some light research on chemistry experiments online and do a search for simple science experiments. Choose an experiment that sounds interesting and prepare a lab report that includes an introduction, the materials you would need, and the steps you would follow. Then guess at the data or results you may find. Review the ways to take guesses or express certainty in Unit 4 and incorporate those into your report.

Vocabulary Log

To increase your vocabulary knowledge, write a definition or translation for each vocabulary item. Then write an original phrase, sentence, or note that will help you remember the vocabulary item.

Vocabulary Item	Definition or Translation	Your Original Phrase, Sentence, or Note
1. abundant	many, a lot	an abundant supply of money
2. a chain		
3. throughout		
4. petroleum		
5. extent		
6. reverse (v.)		
7. aids		
8. coral		
9. a bin		
10. stabilize		
11. versus		
12. flourish		
13. an item		

Vocabulary Item	Definition or Translation	Your Original Phrase, Sentence, or Note
14. shift (v.)		
15. the impact		
16. a surface		
17. visualize		
18. an athlete		
19. remind		
20. a reef		
21. behave		
22. ammonia		
23. the rate		
24. emerge		
25. adjacent		

6

Fine Arts: Arts Appreciation

Art takes many forms, including photography, sculpture, or painting. Different people like different kinds of art. Art appreciation is learning about the art and understanding qualities that make it art. You can look at art from a variety of time periods, artists, and styles and learn to appreciate each piece in its own way, even if you don't like it.

Part 1: Sculptures

Pre-Listening Activities

Sculptures are pieces of art that are 3-D (three-dimensional). Many cultures have a form of sculpture, but they vary in style, color, or history. One thing most sculptures have in common is material. Sculptures are often made from a hard material such as stone, metal, or plastic. Because of that, many sculptures last a long time even if they are outside and exposed to bad weather. Answer these questions with a partner.

1. Do you recognize the sculptures? What are they? Where are they located? What are they made from?

   _____

   _____

   _____

2. What other famous statues can you think of? Where are they? Can you find out what they are made of?

   _____

   _____

   _____

3. What do you appreciate about each statue that you talked about?

   _____

   _____

   _____

Strategy: Listening for and Making General Statements

Sometimes speakers will make generalizations. To make a generalization is to put many things or ideas into one category. Sometimes you need to remember that a general statement is sometimes based on limited facts. It is important to recognize when someone is making a generalization so that you can get more information later if you need to. General statements are sometimes very helpful when they are based on facts or statistics. It helps to make general statements when you are trying to understand broad concepts or remember categories for a test or project. There are some phrases that are used **before** someone makes a general statement.

Making General Statements

    As a rule
    Basically
    Broadly
    By and large
    Generally
    In general
    Typically
    Usually

Words to Include (for Generalizations)

    a majority of
    [almost] always
    [nearly] all
    many
    most
    never
    often

<u>Pronunciation Note</u>: Several generalization words end in *–ly*. In some words, when you add a suffix, the syllable you stress changes (′E-du-cate → e-du-′CA-tion). That is not true for *–ly* endings. The pronunciation of *–ly* words is easy because the stress remains on the same syllable as the word without the suffix. You simply pronounce the *–ly* word with the stress on the same syllable as the base/original word.

    generally → **gen**erally   **us**ually → **us**ually

Reading

Read about the wax sculptures of Edgar Degas (day-gah).

The Degas Waxes:
An Opportunity for In-Depth Investigation

(1) The National Gallery of Art's extensive collection of wax sculptures by Edgar Degas presents a rare opportunity for the investigation of his unconventional approach to sculpture and an in-depth study of much of his work in this genre.

(2) While Degas exhibited only one sculpture in his lifetime—*Little Dancer Aged Fourteen*—more than 100 of the so-called "wax" sculptures were found in his studio after his death. Most are constructed from a mixture of beeswax and modeling clay, with additives such as starches, fats, or resins, and coupled with materials such as corks, paper, rope, and plaster-saturated rags. They are formed over skeletons of wire, wood, metal pins, and other materials. Historical records indicate that only about 30 of these sculptures were intact and suitable for casting in bronze when they were originally discovered, but ultimately bronzes were cast of 74 sculptures, implying that approximately 44 were repaired or enhanced prior to casting.

(3) Of the 70 remaining original sculptures (four were destroyed during the casting process), 50 have come to the Gallery through the generosity of Mr. and Mrs. Paul Mellon. Seventeen were donated in 1985 and 33 more in 1999, giving the Gallery the largest collection of Degas wax sculptures in the world and the majority of the work the artist produced in this medium over a period of approximately 50 years. This remarkable collection, and the Gallery's wide array of scientific resources, afford the museum an opportunity to explore Degas' sculptural techniques and his progression as a sculptor. It also allows for an in-depth analysis of the materials he used and a comparison of their current state to their condition in Degas' day. In addition, the presence of so many Degas sculptures in the collection makes it possible to study which works may have undergone changes after the artist's death and the extent and impact of these revisions. A detailed understanding of the materials used to create the sculptures has already

enhanced conservation efforts; we know the ideal temperature and humidity in which they should be displayed and the materials with which they can safely be repaired. The Gallery's research is also yielding a systematic catalogue devoted to Degas' sculptures, which will enable the Gallery to share its knowledge of these exquisite works of art and the artist's process with conservators, scholars, and connoisseurs around the world. . . .

(4) As a first step toward understanding the waxes, conservators examine each sculpture individually and compare it to historical records, which often exist in the form of photographs. Many, though not all, of the waxes were photographed in an inventory taken in 1917, shortly after Degas' death. A comparison of the photograph and the sculpture often reveals subtle changes that have occurred over time; sometimes the changes are drastic. For example, it is clear from such a comparison that *Seated Woman Wiping Her Left Hip* was altered: the 1917 inventory photograph shows a headless figure, while the existing wax sculpture includes the figure's head. . . .

(5) X-rays taken of the Degas waxes in the Gallery's collection have revealed many intriguing facts about his work. They show, for instance, that there is a lack of a significant skeleton in some of the pieces, an aspect of Degas' work for which he was criticized by his contemporaries. X-radiography has also revealed the presence of many unusual objects used as internal support, including a drafting tool, paint brushes, chunks of wood, wine bottle corks, and even a perforated lid. The pins shown on the x-rays often provide clues as to which of the sculptures have been repaired. Conservators and historians have determined the materials Degas typically used for the skeletons; the presence of other materials is a clear indication of a restorer's work. Although none of the pieces other than *Little Dancer Aged Fourteen* is dated, the researchers speculate that those with more highly defined skeleton preceded those in which little armature exists.

(6) Often research such as that being undertaken on the Degas waxes is intended, in part, to establish the authenticity of the works, yet the authenticity of the waxes is not in question. There is uncertainty, however, about where Degas' work begins and ends, since it is known that many of the waxes were repaired or otherwise altered after his death.

Excerpted and adapted from National Gallery of Art, *The Degas Waxes*, 2011.

Listening for and Making Generalizations

Look at the reading again. Use a highlighter to mark information that you think is general (applies to a lot of or most of Degas's sculptures). Choose another color of highlighter to mark information or words that you think is more specific. Don't worry about understanding all the words. What is important is that you realize when speakers are generalizing and when they are giving specific details. When you finish, work with a partner to answer the questions.

1. Can you find three pieces of information to put in the chart?

Generalizations	Specifics

2. What words are used that helped you decide the author was making generalizations?

_____

_____

_____

3. What other reasons did you have for recognizing general versus specific information?

_____

_____

_____

Listening 1: Listening for Generalizations

Listening for Information

The listening passage is the introduction to a tour at an art museum. The tour guide is giving some information about sculptures. Some of the information is about sculptures in general. Other information is about specific examples or facts. As you listen to the conversation, write answers to the questions.

Listening for Information

1. Can you recognize when the tour guide is making generalizations and when she is giving specific information? Write a G next to the generalizations and S next to specific information.

   a. _____ chests and shoulders are part of a bust

   b. _____ equestrian statues were made in the 1850s

   c. _____ statues are made from traditional materials

   d. _____ sculptures made out of bicycle parts

   e. _____ sculpture materials are durable

2. What vocabulary was used to make generalizations?

   _____

   _____

3. What types of materials did the tour guide give as general information?

   _____

   _____

Speaking

Expressing a Positive or Negative Reactions

Sometimes you need to give someone a positive or negative answer. There are many ways to express those. Some are stronger than simply saying yes or no. Others are weaker. Others are formal, while some are informal.

EXPRESSING POSITIVE OR NEGATIVE REACTIONS

Yes	No
Yes.	No.
Yep.	Nope.
Uh-huh.	Un-uhh.
Sure.	Not so much.
Mostly.	Not really.
It's OK.	Not especially.
Sort of.	Not even a little.
Absolutely.	Not at all.
Definitely.	No way.

Expressing Positive or Negative Reactions

Think about times when you have had to give a positive or negative reaction. Then share your ideas with the class.

1. How would you respond if you were asked about each of these things?

   a. a friend's painting:

      you like it _____

      you hate it _____

   b. a Rodin sculpture:

      you like it _____

      you hate it _____

   c. your instructor's lecture:

      you like it _____

      you hate it _____

   d. a new best-selling novel:

      you like it _____

      you hate it _____

   e. your mom's dinner:

      you like it _____

      you hate it _____

   Rank the terms in the box on page 169 from strongest to weakest. Compare your answers with another group.

   _____

   _____

   _____

   _____

2. What words do you use to give positive reactions? To give negative reactions? Add other phrases to the list and to the box on page 169.

_____

_____

_____

3. What things affect the strength of your response? Does the place or time of the interaction matter? Does it matter who you are talking to or what you are talking about?

_____

_____

_____

 ## Making Contact

Choose three greetings from the list on page 8, and greet three different English speakers. Find a picture of a sculpture. It can be any sculpture you want. Show it to three English speakers. Ask them if they like it. Take notes on the greeting you used, the response you received, and the details of the interaction (person's status, age, and gender, the time of day, and the location). Be prepared to discuss your data with the class.

Person's Response	Positive or Negative?	Details of the Interaction

Part 2: Painting

Pre-Listening Activities

Part 1 talked about sculptures, which are three-dimensional. Part 2 is about another form of art, but one that is 1-D or one-dimensional. Painting is using a brush to add paint, or some sort of color, onto a surface. The word *painting* is a noun, but it has two meanings. It is both the actual act of applying the paint, and it is the result of the act. Answer these questions with a partner.

1. Which painting do you like best? What do you appreciate about it?

   _____

   _____

   _____

2. Can you think of any famous paintings? List as many as you can. Talk about why you think they are famous. Where are they located? Who were the artists?

   _____

   _____

   _____

3. What is the most interesting painting you've seen? Was it in a museum or did someone you know paint it. Why did you like it?

   _____

   _____

   _____

Strategy: Listening for and Giving Additional Reasons

In lectures and academic discussions, and even in casual conversations, speakers will give more than one reason for their opinion or idea. Giving reasons makes your statements stronger. Certain words and phrases indicate that another reason is coming, especially at the beginning of a sentence. Listening for these will help you understand better.

Giving Additional Reasons

Also,

And,

Another thing,

Besides that,

Furthermore,

I mean

In addition,

Not only, but also

One more thing,

Plus,

> You want to look at Chinese paintings from the Ming Dynasty because artists then used more colors than in earlier Chinese paintings. **Furthermore**, artists from this period began experimenting with new skills.

> We're going to write about Leonardo da Vinci. **Not only** was he a painter, **but** he was **also** a sculptor.

Pronunciation Note: **Reduction** is when sounds are reduced or dropped in spoken English. Sometimes two words sound like one. For example, *wanna* is a reduction of *want to*.

> You **wanna** look at Chinese paintings from the Ming Dynasty because artists then used more colors than in earlier Chinese paintings.

> We're **gonna** write about Leonardo da Vinci.

Listening for and Giving Additional Reasons

Complete each sentence. Then write a second sentence that begins with an additional signal word or phrase and another reason.

1. My favorite class is _____ because _____.

   _____, _____

   _____.

2. I want to be a(n) _____ because _____.

   _____, _____

   _____.

3. The best painting I've seen is _____ because _____.

   _____, _____

   _____.

4. A great museum is _____ because _____.

   _____, _____

   _____.

5. An amazing sculpture is _____ because _____.

   _____, _____

   _____.

Speaking

Making Yourself Clear

Sometimes speakers will say something that isn't clear. Or, they may say something incorrectly. In either case, they can make themselves clear by saying it again in other words or with correct information. There are certain phrases you can use before you make yourself clear. These phrases let your listeners know you are repeating or correcting something you said.

Repeating
I mean
I'm saying that
I'm trying to say
In other words
Let me rephrase that
To put it another way
What I am trying to say is

Making Yourself Clear

Read the excerpted paragraphs from *The Degas Waxes: An Opportunity for In-Depth Investigation*. Choose one sentence from each paragraph, and rewrite both of them to make them clearer for someone. Write your sentences on page 177. Remember that you only have to reword the parts you think are especially hard to understand. Then compare your statements with those of a partner.

(1) *Little Dancer Aged Fourteen*, the only wax sculpture Degas ever exhibited and the most famous of these works, raises numerous questions the Gallery is investigating. "One of our questions is whether the tutu is original. We are comparing it to the inventory photographs, and we will conduct research about the materials from which it is made," says Barbour. "We will also investigate the composition of her slippers, and the wig over which Degas placed wax to form the figure's hair. The wig has always been described as being made of horse hair, but as far as we know no one has ever analyzed it. We can do that now, with the help of our scientific research department, using the Gallery's scanning electron microscope." This microscope, says organic chemist Suzanne Lomax, is capable of high magnification, as well as aiding in material identification. "We can focus on individual particles, and an x-ray spectrometer inside the microscope can tell us what elements are present in that particle."

(2) The scanning electron microscope (SEM) has been particularly helpful in providing information about the composition of the pigments Degas used to tint the wax figures, and the information from these analyses complements the results for pigment identification using polarized light microscopy. [. . .] In addition to the SEM, the Gallery's scientific research department uses another instrument, an x-ray fluorescence spectrometer (XRF), to examine the pigmentation of the wax sculptures. This device is capable of providing information on the composition of the surface of an object without the need for taking a sample. "A beam of x-rays pointed at the work of art interacts with the atoms in the piece, enabling you to obtain a characteristic spectrum from which you can identify the elemental composition of the surface material," explains senior conservation scientist Barbara Berrie.

Excerpted from National Gallery of Art, *The Degas Waxes*, 2011.

1. _____
   _____
   _____
   _____
   _____

2. _____
   _____
   _____
   _____
   _____

Listening 2: Discussing Art

Listening in Groups (Video)

Listen to the students work together to prepare for a test in their art class.

Focus on Language

1. Did any of the students make generalizations? What words did they use to let you know it was a generalization? <u>Note</u>: Refer to the box on page 164. You do not need to use exact words.

    _____

    _____

2. What examples of expressing positive and negative reactions did you hear? Which do you think were stronger? Refer to the box on page 169. <u>Note</u>: You do not need to use exact words.

    _____

    _____

3. What words or phrases do the students use before adding another reason? What words do they use? <u>Note</u>: You do not need to use exact words.

    _____

    _____

4. How did the students try to make themselves clearer? <u>Note</u>: You do not need to use exact words.

    _____

    _____

5. Write any phrases or idioms that you are not familiar with. Discuss what they mean and in what type of interactions they are appropriate.

    _____

    _____

Focus on Tone

1. How can you tell how each person is feeling about the artwork being discussed?

   _____

   _____

2. Which positive reactions were strongest? Negative?

   _____

   _____

3. Is each person's tone appropriate? Why or why not?

   _____

   _____

Focus on Nonverbal Communication

1. What nonverbal cues are used to show how each member of the group feels about the artwork being discussed?

   _____

   _____

2. Were any of these inappropriate? Why or why not?

   _____

   _____

3. Which student do you think has the most expressive nonverbal communication? Is this good or bad for the interaction?

   _____

   _____

Summary

1. Which piece of art do you think you would like best?

   _____

   _____

   _____

   _____

2. Which student uses the best combination of words, tone, and nonverbal communication? Support your answer.

   _____

   _____

   _____

   _____

3. Who would you most want to work with? Why? Who would you rather not work with? Why?

   _____

   _____

   _____

   _____

Ranking

Have you visited a museum? What do you consider when deciding which museums to visit in other cities? *The Art Magazine* compiled a list of the museums with the highest attendance. Any museum with any type of art was included. What do you think the museums had that attracted so many visitors?

Qualities of a Good Museum

_____

_____

_____

_____

Read this list of 18 museums. What do you think are the top 3 and bottom 3 in terms of attendance. When you finish, discuss what each of your top 3 museums has that makes it such a popular tourist destination.

British Museum, London
Centre Georges Pompidou, Paris
Hermitage Museum, Saint Petersburg
Metropolitan Museum of Art, New York City
Musee d'Orsay, Paris
Musee du Louvre, Paris
Museo del Prado, Madrid
Museo Nacional Centro de Arte Reina Sofia, Madrid
National Gallery of Art, Washington, DC
National Gallery, United Kingdom
National Museum of Korea, Seoul
National Palace Museum, Taipei
Tate Modern, London
Tokyo National Museum, Tokyo
Victoria and Albert Museum, London

Our Ranking

Top 3	Bottom 3
_____ _____ _____	
Explain your ranking:	**Explain your ranking:**

Part 3: Photography

Pre-Listening Activities

Parts 1 and 2 talked about types of art that most often come to mind when talking about art appreciation. This part is about photography, art capturing objects in still or moving pictures. Although many people use photography to take pictures of special moments, people, or places, some artists capture images that are placed in museums and galleries to be appreciated by many. Answer these questions with a partner.

1. Do you like to take pictures? What do you take pictures of?

   _____

   _____

   _____

2. What qualities does a photograph need to contain to be appreciated?

   _____

   _____

   _____

3. What is the subject of a favorite photograph you have seen (personal or professional). What did you like about it?

   _____

   _____

   _____

Strategy: Listening for and Using Main Idea Signal Words and Phrases

Many formal lectures and speeches contain main idea words. Speakers will use these words to let their listeners know what the main ideas are. These are ideas you want to mark in your notes or organize into a main idea chart when you are studying. When you hear a main idea word, it usually means more than one of something. These sentences are usually main ideas and prepare you for subpoints and details that will likely follow.

Main Idea Signal Words and Phrases

a few key [points]

several [types]

among the [factors]

various [ideas]

numerous [advantages]

four [laws]

series [of steps]

examples [of places]

Other Phrases

Why should you know this?

Remember

What's important is

Photography production can be divided into **four** categories.

I'll talk about the history of photography during **several** time periods.

Various photographers have made their mark in the art field.

I found **numerous** results based on how a picture is developed.

I have **a few** key points to make during today's lecture.

Using Main Idea Signal Words and Phrases

Look at each set of subpoints from a lecture on art appreciation. Write a main idea using a main point signal from the box on page 184 or another one you think is appropriate. The first two have been done for you as an examples. Don't worry if you get the main idea correct, concentrate on the main idea words.

1. sculptures, paintings, photographs = _three types of art_____

2. black and white, color, digital = _various kinds of photographs_____

3. ancient art, 18th century art, modern art = _____

4. Monet, Rembrandt, Michelangelo = _____

5. people, fruit baskets, mountains = _____

6. Italy, France, Spain = _____

7. music, literature, film = _____

8. plastic, metal, stone = _____

✏ Note-Taking

Strategy: Using a Main Idea Table

A main idea table is a good way to take notes or organize your notes after a lecture. You can record the main idea phrases in the left column and the details or examples in the right column. Your main idea table can be as simple or as detailed as you want.

If you were to create a main idea table for the items in the activity on page 185, the top of your chart might look like this.

Main Ideas	Details
three types of art	sculptures paintings photographs

Developing a Main Idea Table

Think of main ideas and subpoints or details for categories in your own field of study. Create a main idea table with three main ideas and three subpoints for each one. Share your main idea charts with a small group.

Vocabulary Power

There are a number of terms and phrases in this lecture that you may encounter in other academic settings. Add at least five vocabulary items to your vocabulary notebook or log.

Match the words in bold from the lecture on the left with a definition on the right.

1. _____ Other types of commercial photographers include fashion photographers or the paparazzi—you know, those photographers who **capture** images of famous movie stars at the airport or around town.

    a. insect

    b. show

    c. from left to right

2. _____ Artists take pictures for the purpose of art, to have their photographs **displayed** in a museum.

    d. discuss briefly

3. _____ There are various **techniques** photographers can use.

    e. where two lines cross

4. _____ Think of some of the photographs you see in a science textbook; those in which you can see the very fine details of the **bug**.

    f. take

    g. method; way

5. _____ We don't have much time left, but I want to **touch on** numerous technical aspects of photography that photographers need to consider.

    h. whole; complete

6. _____ It might be that the **entire** image is clearly seen.

7. _____ The most important elements in the photograph should fall along those those imaginary lines or at their **intersections**.

8. _____ Now draw two **horizontal** lines. Again, one should be one-third from the top and the other should be one-third from the bottom.

Listening 3: Photography

Listening to a Lecture

The listening passage is a lecture from an art appreciation class on photography. The instructor is giving an overview of photography. The lecturer uses several main idea signal words and phrases. As you listen, take notes. Then try to organize your notes into a main idea table. Use a separate sheet of paper.

Checking Your Understanding: Main Ideas

Review your notes and main idea table. Listen again to the lecture if necessary, and then put a check mark (✔) next to the statements that best reflect the main ideas.

1. _____ There are several kinds of photographers.

2. _____ There are many types of fine art photography.

3. _____ Photographers use various techniques.

4. _____ Many kinds of special equipment are required.

5. _____ There are numerous technical aspects of photography.

Checking Your Understanding: Details

Use your notes and main idea table, and put a check mark (✓) next to the best answer. Some questions have more than one answer.

1. What types of photographers are mentioned?

   a. _____ aerial

   b. _____ amateurs

   c. _____ panoramic

   d. _____ commercial

2. What are various techniques photographers can use?

   a. _____ macro

   b. _____ exposure

   c. _____ fine art

   d. _____ aerial

   e. _____ panoramic

3. What are technical aspects of photography?

   a. _____ how an object looks from the sky

   b. _____ how long an object is

   c. _____ amount of light allowed

   d. _____ sharpness of an image

4. What is true about the rule of thirds?

   a. _____ Elements should fall along the lines.

   b. _____ Elements should fall in the bottom third.

   c. _____ Elements should fall between the lines.

   d. _____ Elements should fall in all nine squares.

In-Depth Discussion

Work with a small group. Imagine you work for a publishing company and that you want to publish a book of photographs. Answer the questions and then present your publishing plan to the class.

1. What kind of photographs will you use (color, black and white, etc.)?

   _____

   _____

2. What kind of subjects will your book cover (people, places, things, etc.)? Be specific.

   _____

   _____

3. What characteristics of the photographs do you want people to appreciate?

   _____

   _____

4. What would be the most unique photograph?

   _____

   _____

5. What kind of book is it (hard cover, coffee table book, etc.)

   _____

   _____

6. How much does it cost?

   _____

   _____

7. Where will it be sold?

   _____

   _____

8. Who is your target audience?

   _____

   _____

Rapid Vocabulary Review

From the three answers on the right, circle the one that best explains, is an example of, or combines with the vocabulary item on the left as it is used in this unit.

Vocabulary	Answers		
Synonyms			
1. literal	exact	likely	somewhat
2. current	past	present	future
3. as a rule	always	in general	rarely
4. intriguing	interesting	a large number of	ruling
5. a series of	one	several	zero
6. statistics	numbers	opinions	predictions
7. subdivisions	parts	two halves	one whole
8. donate	give	like	move
9. authentic	final	possible	real
10. enhance	believe	improve	get
11. perforated	with details	with friends	with holes
12. broad	masculine	thinking	wide
Combinations and Associations			
13. be in ___	answer	question	idea
14. ___ inventory	take	make	choose
15. what I meant to ___	say	speak	tell
16. be ___ to	based	exposed	various
17. clear something ___	in	on	up
18. the current ___	airplane	state	ocean
19. be ___ with	familiar	key	rather
20. a ___ of	lack	legal	lid

⇨⟩⟨⇦ Synthesizing: Projects and Presentations

Short In-Class Speaking Assignments	Longer Outside Assignments
Categories	**Museum Research**
Work with a partner to make lists of main ideas and subpoints or details for the different topics/disciplines in this book. Then, read your list. Can the rest of the class guess the main idea.	Do light research on one of the Top 15 Most Visited Museums. Prepare a short presentation about the museum. Consider including details about what artists are exhibited there, famous pieces of art, and other details that may be reasons why it is a popular museum. Give your presentation to the rest of the class.
Give Me a Reason	**Art Appreciation**
Work with a partner. Take turns naming things you see around you or know about. Ask your partner for a reaction (positive or negative). Your partner will give a reaction and two reasons for the reaction. Some things you can name include colors, restaurants, food items, pieces of art, different classes, vacation spots, sports, television shows, or movies.	Find a picture of a piece of art you like. Prepare a presentation about the artwork. Your presentation may include main ideas and details about the history, characteristics, or artist. Include generalizations about the time period or type of art and explain why this piece belongs in that category. End your presentation by asking your classmates for their reactions to the artwork you chose.

Vocabulary Log

To increase your vocabulary knowledge, write a definition or translation for each vocabulary item. Then write an original phrase, sentence, or note that will help you remember the vocabulary item.

Vocabulary Item	Definition or Translation	Your Original Phrase, Sentence, or Note
1. key	main, most important	a key idea
2. a sculpture		
3. a material		
4. remarkable		
5. numerous		
6. a genre		
7. indicate		
8. a target		
9. contemporaries		
10. intriguing		
11. enable		
12. rags		
13. alter (v.)		

Vocabulary Item	Definition or Translation	Your Original Phrase, Sentence, or Note
14. speculate		
15. slippers		
16. intact		
17. subtle		
18. extensive		
19. ideal		
20. nearly		
21. clear up		
22. by and large		
23. typically		
24. share (v.)		
25. prior to		